Resilience of an African Giant

Resilience of an African Giant

*Boosting Growth and Development in
the Democratic Republic of Congo*

Johannes Herderschee
Kai-Alexander Kaiser
Daniel Mukoko Samba

THE WORLD BANK
Washington, D.C.

ISBN: 978-0-8213-8909-6
eISBN: 978-0-8213-8910-2
DOI: 10.1596/978-0-8213-8909-6

Library of Congress Cataloging-in-Publication Data
Herderschee, Han.
  Resilience of an African giant : boosting growth and development in the Democratic Republic of Congo / Johannes Herderschee, Kai-Alexander Kaiser, Daniel Mukoko Samba.
    p. cm.
  Includes bibliographical references and index.
  ISBN 978-0-8213-8909-6 — ISBN 978-0-8213-8910-2 (electronic)
  1. Congo (Democratic Republic)—Economic conditions—1960- 2. Congo (Democratic Republic)—Economic policy. 3. Economic development—Congo (Democratic Republic) I. Kaiser, Kai-Alexander. II. Mukoko Samba, Daniel. III. World Bank. IV. Title.
  HC955.H47 2011
  338.96751—dc23

                                                                                2011038070

Cover photograph: Macaire Tshiala Bongo / The World Bank
Cover illustration: Jeffrey Lecksell / The World Bank
Cover design: Naylor Design

Contents

Boxes

Figures

Foreword

This book pulls together an impressive body of research on the exemplary transition of a country from a state of conflict to a postconflict situation, and from there toward becoming a country with legitimate institutions created by free, democratic, and transparent elections.

The reader's attention will most certainly be drawn to the occasionally candid manner in which the facts contained in this book are presented. This serves, in particular, to augment one's frame of reference and help the reader better grasp the nature of the issues confronted by all development actors.

The detailed analysis of administrative, political, and economic governance over the past 20 years facilitates a better understanding of the context and the fragile situations faced by the Democratic Republic of Congo. Without ever deferring to the Government in any way, the authors highlight the failures and successes amassed on the development front. Through the quality of their work and the accuracy of their statements, they offer us the opportunity to begin thoughtful discussions about the policies to be adopted in order to achieve the development outcomes that are much anticipated by the Congolese people.

As the Minister of Planning and the former President of the National Assembly, I found this book to be particularly interesting as it calls for a hard look at the way matters of State are broached. It urges us to abandon egotism, to repudiate self interest in favor of the search for the common good, and to cultivate a sense of nationhood. In this way, this book may well constitute an invitation to a true revolution of mentalities. I therefore wholeheartedly recommend it to all who are interested in development, particularly to policy makers in my country, as well as its partners.

Olivier Kamitatu Etsu
Minister of Planning, Democratic Republic of Congo

Preface

A stable, peaceful, and prosperous Democratic Republic of Congo promises to have transformational impacts not only for the country's 67 million citizens but also for the entire subregion. Indeed, the Democratic Republic of Congo is the largest country in Sub-Saharan Africa by land area and the third largest in population. At a crossroad between West-Central Africa and East-Southern Africa, it is a neighbor of the East African Community (more than 130 million inhabitants) and a member of the vast Southern African Development Community (260 million inhabitants). Therefore, the country's fortunes are potentially integral to the broader fortunes of the entire continent. But the hopes will only materialize if the country is able to boost its growth and development significantly through effective leadership.

This book analyzes the economic development of the Democratic Republic of Congo in recent years and highlights the major challenges that the country needs to confront in order to promote growth and shared prosperity in the years to come. It is my hope that this comprehensive analytical work and development policy review will constitute an accessible reference and a rich source of information and guidance to Congolese policy makers as well as to international development partners and a wider audience of development practitioners and scholars.

I write this preface as my four-year tenure as the World Bank's country director based in Kinshasa comes to an end, and I use this opportunity to reflect on what I have learned together with my colleagues and Congolese counterparts. These have been both exciting and challenging times, as we have had to design policies that are essential and rigorous enough to strengthen the Democratic Republic of Congo's economic foundations and yet realistic enough to be embraced and effectively implemented in a vast and poor country that faces the daunting tasks of improving governance and consolidating peace. I find this book particularly helpful in this balancing act, as it offers a set of practical and evidence-based contributions to policy design and dialogue in a fragile country.

The national authorities are the main interlocutor of the World Bank. Hence, like many of my colleagues, I have had the great pleasure of working closely with the authorities. However, the task of a country director is in some respects different in the Democratic Republic of Congo than in other countries. The main obstacle to development is not so much the divergence of views with the collective authorities, but the challenge for the national authorities of agreeing on a collective position in front of external parties, as documented in this book.

As country director, one of my tasks has been to use the convening power of the World Bank to facilitate the forging of common positions on various issues among those who control or influence policies in the Democratic Republic of Congo. This has been challenging but also rewarding, thanks to its visible impact on the lives of millions of Congolese and the personal warmth and commitment of my counterparts.

The last five years have also marked the transition of the Democratic Republic of Congo from a centralized state to a decentralized state where major functions of government have been transferred to provincial authorities. I am glad that the Bank has made a significant contribution to this process. Indeed, during my tenure, I visited all of the provincial capitals as well as many rural areas, which gave me a unique opportunity to observe the decentralization process at close hand. While recognizing that technical assistance from the World Bank and other partners may have contributed, it is also clear that underlying forces have been purely Congolese: there has been strong demand for decentralized public services at all levels. The 2006 constitution created important institutions that allows citizens to express this demand and encourage public officials to respond. The book documents the progress that the Democratic

Republic of Congo has made along this road but also highlights the significant challenges remaining.

The road ahead will not be easy, but I am optimistic about the future of this strategic and resourceful nation in the heart of the continent. My optimism is partly based on the facts and analyses presented in this book. There is no doubt that the instruments listed are important: a national consensus, technology, external anchors, and social accountability all play a role. But my most important reason for optimism is the commitment of the Congolese people to coming together to build a strong nation for shared prosperity. The Democratic Republic of Congo has the necessary resources for that goal; what it needs most is a collective resolve stirred by stronger governance to lead the way.

Marie Françoise Marie-Nelly
Country Director for the Democratic Republic of Congo
January 2008–September 2011
World Bank

Acknowledgments

Generous support from development partners of the Democratic Republic of Congo allowed the commissioning of 14 background studies that covered new ground and collected original data. A trade facilitation audit was funded by the Multi-Donor Trade Facilitation Trust Fund administered by the World Bank. That audit also benefited from a contribution from the French Development Agency. The results of the trade facilitation audit were integrated and elaborated into the Diagnostic Trade Integration Study, which benefited from funding provided by the Enhanced Integrated Framework Secretariat at the World Trade Organization. Detailed studies on the prospects for regional integration in the Great Lakes region and the Kinshasa-Brazzaville metropolitan area were generously funded by a Trade Policy Trust Fund administered by the Africa Vice Presidency of the World Bank. In parallel, the Swedish International Development Agency provided generous funding for a growth diagnostic study that covered five provinces. The results presented in that report were developed further thanks to funding from the Multi-Donor Growth Diagnostic Trust Fund. The Belgium Poverty Reduction Partnership Trust Fund supported assistance to help the Congolese provinces to formulate their budgets and prepare Poverty Reduction Strategy Papers. That task required the collection of data on economic activities that also informed the analytical work reported in this study. Thanks to support from the United States Agency for International Development, the estimates of economic activities in the 11 provinces were discussed in a workshop in Kinshasa. The World Bank Investment Climate Assessment Unit funded a new survey of business establishments in the Democratic Republic of Congo in 2010. The Belgium Poverty Reduction Partnership Trust Fund generously provided resources that contributed to the background paper on urbanization issues as well as funding to make the background papers available to Congolese audiences. The Governance Partnership Facility contributed to the cost of publishing this book in the Directions in Development series.

This report synthesizes the 14 background studies and also draws on the results of the Diagnostic Trade Integration Study that was completed in mid-2010. The topics of the background studies were selected consistent with the advice of the concept paper review meeting that was held on December 17, 2008, which benefited from the recommendations of the reviewers Roumeen Islam and Farrukh Iqbal. The review meeting's recommendation to focus on political economy and governance issues shaped the terms of reference of the background studies. This emphasis is also reflected in the synthesis report.

The report responds to a request from the Congolese authorities. Congolese economists contributed to the study, many of whom are co-authors of background papers. The study has benefited from discussion with many policy makers and observers. Suggestions from Dieudonné Manu Essimbo and François Kabuya Kalala, national coordinators of the Technical Committee of Reforms 2002–10 and 2010–11, respectively, were particularly helpful.

Jan Walliser (sector manager, AFTP3) and Marie Françoise Marie-Nelly (country director) provided overall guidance and support. World Bank Vice President for the Africa Region Obiageli Katryn Ezekwesili provided vision and leadership and set the tone for the country dialogue. Hinh Dinh and Eric Bell (Poverty Reduction and Economic Management Unit lead economist and cluster leader in 2008–09 and 2009–11, respectively) advised on how to frame the story line of the report. Phil Keefer and Tony Verheijen advised on political economy and governance issues. Markus Scheuermaier contributed to the historical and long-term growth perspective. Anne Mossige and Johan Verhaghe drafted the boxes on, respectively, the experience with social programs and the public-private partnership in the education sector. Evariste Niyonkuru contributed to the discussion of governance in infrastructure. Bernard Harborne and Mohammed Bekhechi contributed, respectively, to the sections on security issues and legal reform. Nathaniel Arnold (IMF) advised on the presentation of some of the fiscal data. Doerte Doemeland and Bernard Harborne provided comments on the structure of the draft, pointing to missing pieces.

The report was discussed at a World Bank decision meeting on March 29, 2011. Comments by peer reviewers Bernard Hoekman, Punam Chuhan-Pole, and Professor James Robinson, in addition to the lively discussion at the meeting itself, helped to clarify the focus and policy recommendations.

The synthesis report and all background studies have benefited from the active contribution of all members of the Democratic Republic of Congo country team. Detailed comments on the synthesis report were received from Steven Dimitriyev, Alexandre Dossou, Philippe Durand, Julien Galant, Daria Goldstein, Shiho Nagaki, Vincent Palmade, Remi Pelon, Rachidi Radji, Christophe Rockmore, Markus Scheuermaier, Silvana Tordo, and Tony Verheijen.

Janine Mans (2008–10) and Shiho Nagaki (2009–11) helped to manage the project, selecting consultants, preparing terms of reference, and keeping the process on track. World Bank resident economists Emilie Mushobekwa and Moïse Tshimenga provided valuable advice. Chloë Domergue, consultant at IDEA International, edited the synthesis report and supported the management of the final stages of the project. Mariama Daifour Ba, Lucie Bobola, and Paula White provided expert assistance at every stage of the project. The background papers have their own authors, as acknowledged in each of the volumes in which the papers have been compiled. This report has been translated into French by an IDEA International team, under the supervision of Chloë Domergue and reviewed by Marie Elisabeth Camus and Jérôme Chevalier. Lucie Bobola managed the dissemination events in June and September 2011.

This book has benefited from comments received during a public discussion of a draft Country Economic Memorandum with Congolese authorities at the Democratic Republic of Congo Ministry of Foreign Affairs on June 7, 2011. The event was opened by the vice prime minister in charge of telecommunications, His Excellency Simon Bulupiy Galati, and the World Bank country director, Marie Françoise Marie-Nelly. The section on governance was moderated by Patrick Kitebi, adviser to the minister of finance, with discussants former ministers Général Denis Kalume (via a representative) and Gilbert Kiakwama (member of Parliament for the opposition). His Excellency Olivier Kamitatu, Minister of Planning, and Marcelo Giugale, Director, Poverty Reduction and Economic Management at the World Bank, contributed to the debate. The discussion on infrastructure challenges was moderated by Tobie Chalondawa, director of the Government Project Coordination Unit, with discussants Kimbembe Mazunga, infrastructure adviser to the president, and his Excellency Fridolin Kasweshi, minister of infrastructure. The section on private sector development was moderated by Jean Amisi, economic adviser to the president, with discussants Matipa Mumba, adviser to the minister of planning on business climate issues, and Michel Losembe, director of Citibank and vice president of the Congolese Employer Organization. The event was closed by Daniel Mukoko Samba, co-author and deputy chief of staff to the prime minister, and Jan Walliser, sector manager of the Poverty Reduction and Economic Management Unit at the World Bank.

The publication of this book was managed by Stephen McGroarty, Aziz Gokdemir, Cindy Fisher, and Nora Ridolfi. The cover illustration was prepared by Jeffrey Lecksell, cartographer. The photo was taken by Macaire Tshiala Bongo and selected by Louise Engulu, senior communications officer at the World Bank. It shows the distribution of school books funded by the World Bank PARSE project to support primary and secondary education.

Abbreviations

ATM	automatic teller machine
COPIREP	Comité de Pilotage de la Reforme des Entreprises du Portefeuille de l'État (Committee to Manage the Reform of the Portfolio of State-Owned Enterprises)
EU	European Union
FDI	foreign direct investment
FDLR	Forces Démocratiques de Libération du Rwanda (Democratic Liberation Forces of Rwanda)
FSRDC	Fond Social de la République Démocratique du Congo (Social Fund of the Democratic Republic of Congo)
GDP	gross domestic product
HIPC	heavily indebted poor countries
HVDC	high-voltage direct current
ICA	Investment Climate Assessment
IMF	International Monetary Fund
LIPW	Labor-Intensive Public Works Project
MDRI	Multilateral Debt Relief Initiative
MONUC	Mission des Nations Unies au Congo (United Nations Organization Mission in the Democratic Republic of Congo)

NGO   nongovernmental organization
OCPT   Office Congolais des Postes et Télécommunications
          (state-owned telecommunication and postal company)
OHADA   L'Organisation pour l'Harmonisation en Afrique du Droit
          des Affaires (Organization for the Harmonization of
          Business Law in Africa)
REDD   Reducing Emissions from Deforestation and Forest
          Degradation
RVA   Régie des Voies Aériennes (state-owned enterprise in
          charge of airport facilities and air traffic control)
SCTP   Société Commerciale des Transports et des Ports
          (Commercial Society for Transport and Ports)
SNCC   Société Nationale des Chemins de Fer du Congo
          (National Society for Railways)
SNEL   Société Nationale d'Electricité (National Society for
          Electricity)

Currency Equivalents
(As of December 2010)

Currency = Congolese franc (CGF)
US$1   = CGF 925

System of Measurement
Metric system

Executive Summary

The size, resources, and location of the Democratic Republic of Congo have an impact on all of Central Africa. The country has unexplored mining resources, massive agricultural potential, and a population of more than 60 million inhabitants.[1] The second largest country in Sub-Saharan Africa, the Democratic Republic of Congo borders nine countries and has complex economic, migration, and political relations with each of them. Its development has a significant impact on the economic growth and political stability of the continent.

The international community has a long-standing involvement in the country. During the cold war Western countries supported the Democratic Republic of Congo, despite its poor economic policies and political repression. Following the end of the cold war, foreign interest declined, reemerging around the turn of the century. In the last 10 years, the international community has invested considerable resources to stabilize the country through international peacekeeping efforts. Rising commodity prices have also ignited interest in the country's unexploited natural resources.

A Fragile Recovery

The country still suffers from the impact of a major war during the 1990s. This war had two phases: one in 1996–97 and one in 1998–2002. A period of relative prosperity during 1960–70 was based on copper and other commodity exports, which proved unsustainable when copper prices collapsed in the mid-1970s (see figure ES.1). Lack of investment sapped the potential of the mining sector, and both corporate and public institutions were too weak to absorb the commodity price shock; policies became unsustainable. The country descended rapidly from prosperity to war, with unpaid soldiers ransacking Kinshasa, the nation's capital, in 1991–93, bringing destruction from which the city has not yet recovered. Infrastructure collapsed, and today only four provincial capitals can be reached by road from Kinshasa. Four years later, the country destabilized even further, entering two wars during a six-year period that cost millions of lives.

The end of the second war in 2002 coincided with a recovery in mining prices on international markets. Mines that were closed as a result of nationalization and war were reopened as part of joint ventures with international partners. As mining production increased, so did demand for transport and security services as well as financing for trade and construction projects. Key infrastructure bottlenecks were not addressed, however, and social liabilities blocked the reform of state-owned enterprises. Agricultural and informal sector growth was initially subdued, but picked up after 2006 in those provinces where peace and security had improved.

Poverty remains pervasive. Poverty indicators are high by regional standards: under-five child mortality rates remain at approximately 15 percent, less than a quarter of the population has access to safe drinking water, and less than a tenth of the population has access to electricity.

Figure ES.1   GDP per Capita, 1960–2008

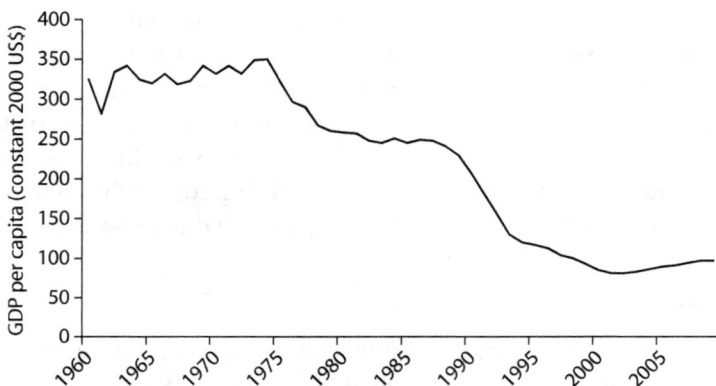

However, poverty outcomes have been improving in recent years. Maternal deaths from childbirth declined from more than 1 percent of live births in 2001 to well below 1 percent in 2008. Primary school enrollment rates increased from 64 to 71 percent between 2005 and 2007. Women remain disadvantaged relative to men, but the inequity is gradually declining. Rapid growth in agricultural production during recent years may have contributed to these favorable outcomes; agriculture creates income-generating opportunities for the poor and reduces food prices, which dominate the low-income consumption basket. Health and education indicators may also have benefited from the involvement of religious organizations and nongovernmental organizations in the health and education sectors.

Income levels may have improved for the poor, but there are few job opportunities for skilled workers. Employment in formal, fully registered companies is rare; the data do not allow precise estimates, but small and medium-sized companies likely employ only 1.2 percent of the workforce. Assuming the total workforce is some 24 million people, this amounts to 300,000 jobs.[2] Employment in established firms appears to have grown only at some 2–3 percent a year; given the growth in the workforce this is insufficient to reduce unemployment. During the same period, some large mining and telecommunications companies have expanded their operations. However, there are few such companies, so this growth has had no significant impact on employment opportunities. Recently collected data suggest that there has been rapid employment growth in small-scale agriculture and the informal sector, but these sectors do not create opportunities for skilled workers. The absence of a dynamic small and medium-size enterprise sector deprives the Democratic Republic of Congo of an important engine of growth and young skilled workers of job opportunities.

The analysis suggests that poor governance stifles the performance of small and medium-size enterprises in the formal sector. Poor governance enables public agencies and officials to impose myriad taxes and levies, both formal and informal, on the private sector. A limited number of large privately owned companies may have managed to insulate themselves from these risks and continue to prosper despite the many operational challenges. Small and medium-size companies have not been able to overcome these obstacles for lack of means and political clout. State-owned enterprises maintain monopoly positions even though they are unable to deliver reliable services. Social liabilities—that is, wage arrears and indemnities—prevent these state-owned enterprises from developing into viable commercial companies.

Governance and the Evolution of Political Institutions

The Democratic Republic of Congo's turbulent history has precluded the development of cohesive elites that agree on economic policy objectives and implementation mechanisms. During his long tenure (1965–97), President Mobutu systematically undermined horizontal networks that could challenge his authority. Outsiders contributed to the lack of social accountability, seeing his regime as a strategic ally against communist-supported Angola and later Zimbabwe. The genocide in Rwanda in 1994 and its aftermath destabilized the Democratic Republic of Congo, and an appeal to ethnic fragmentation fueled conflict at the local level. Large United Nations peacekeeping forces provided some protection and stability, but lasting cooperation among the national elites remains uncertain.

Despite the adoption of a new constitution, the political situation remains fragile. During 2001–05, state effectiveness gradually improved, as armed groups cooperated with each other under an interim constitution. In an effort to make the government more effective and accountable, a new constitution was approved in a referendum and promulgated in February 2006, paving the way for the first democratic elections in 40 years. However, although the constitution mandated stronger provincial governments, the presidency remains the predominant power. Neither state institutions nor the world's largest United Nations peacekeeping forces are strong enough to protect the population from violence. There are considerable inefficiencies at the government level: publicly announced policies are not implemented, and parliamentarily approved budgets are circumvented by procedures to expedite "urgent" expenditures; government agencies are managed as sovereign entities and not as institutions of the state; revenue agencies are paid for mobilizing revenues and not for delivering public services; and some public agencies request payment for services no longer being delivered. The constitution was amended in January 2011, strengthening the position of the president, but the political situation remains fragile. The next elections are scheduled for November 2011.

This fragility was exposed in 2009 when the Democratic Republic of Congo simultaneously experienced an exogenous (commodity price) shock and an endogenous security shock. In 2009 exports of goods and nonfactor services declined 30 percent. Imports contracted 40 percent as financing dried up. In early February 2009 gross foreign exchange reserves were almost completely exhausted. At the same time the authorities were challenged by a rebellion in North Kivu. They responded by taking dramatic action and securing an agreement with Rwanda that included provisions to integrate the North Kivu–based rebels into the regular army. Economic policy was adjusted to satisfy the requirements of the Heavily Indebted Poor Countries (HIPC) Initiative, making the country eligible to receive some US$12 billion in debt relief.

The vulnerability exposed by the 2009 crisis continues to affect the behavior of those who control or influence policy. During the second half of 2009, external pressures eased as mining prices recovered. In 2010 exports and imports of goods and nonfactor services exceeded 2008 levels by 26 and 14 percent, respectively, following their postwar trend. Uncertainty lingered, however, because the crisis had revealed vulnerabilities in the country's economic and security position. Since the crisis, national authorities have increasingly challenged international corporate interests in the natural resource sector, amidst some controversy, and treated telecommunications companies harshly. Trade facilitation procedures have deteriorated, further contributing to costly cross-border procedures, with some of the longest delays in Africa. Harassment and prohibitive informal payments have prevented employment growth by small and medium-size companies.

Overcoming the Governance Challenges

Developments during the past decade have demonstrated the capacity of the Democratic Republic of Congo to achieve positive results under the right conditions. This study points to four positive developments that may support the development of institutional arrangements to address the country's governance challenges: (a) recent agricultural growth, (b) mobile telephone service, (c) external anchors to strengthen legal procedures, and (d) public-private partnerships. In addition, recent legislative activity at the national level illustrates that the government can work effectively and productively with its legislative branch if it allocates sufficient resources to this task. This suggests that the existing institutional arrangements can function as designed.

Agricultural production is increasing rapidly in the provinces, suggesting cooperation among political groups at the provincial level (see table ES.1). Both subsistence farming and production for local markets are growing rapidly in areas where security has been reestablished. This was not the case in both of the Kivu provinces in 2007–08.

The Democratic Republic of Congo is using external anchors to provide greater legal certainty. The upcoming accession to the Organization

Table ES.1   Agricultural Growth, by Data Source, 2007–10

percent

Source	2007	2008	2009	2010
Provincial data	−0.6	6.7	7.0	7.7
Central bank data	3.3	3.0	3.0	3.0

Source: Background paper, III.3.

for the Harmonization of Business Law in Africa Treaty will modernize the country's legal framework. Accession to the New York Arbitration Convention of 1958 is also being considered, and this would be another important step toward judicial transparency and predictability. In addition, there are practical solutions to legal issues. Trade facilitation procedures have been complicated and time-consuming because all agencies prefer to collect their own fees directly from traders. The agencies recently recommended that a single window collect these fees on their behalf, provided this window is administered under credible arrangements by a joint venture that includes national shareholders and a foreign operator subject to international accounting standards. This outcome would contribute to both national capacity and trust among the parties involved. If successful, this model could also be used to establish a national revenue authority, which could replace the myriad competing revenue authorities that currently exist.

Innovative institutional arrangements are being used to build infrastructure. During 2002–08 almost all new infrastructure in the country was constructed by development partners. This changed in 2008, when the Democratic Republic of Congo engaged in a partnership with three Chinese companies supported by the Export Import Bank of China. Their agreement established a joint venture to exploit a specific mining concession; the revenues from that concession will be used to repay the country's investment in mining and the loans contracted to finance the rapid expansion of infrastructure (see figure ES.2). The agreement was negotiated outside regular procedures, and its implementation relies on external—in this case, Chinese—administrative procedures and institutions. The direct involvement of the president and his advisers may have facilitated both the negotiations and implementation of the agreement. Construction of the facilities is ongoing. The institutional arrangements to ensure subsequent maintenance and operations are not clear, but the authorities have indicated that they are considering the use of public-private partnerships.

Public-private partnerships are already being used to deliver public education and health services. The Congolese state has a long-standing

Figure ES.2   Public Investment as a Percent of GDP

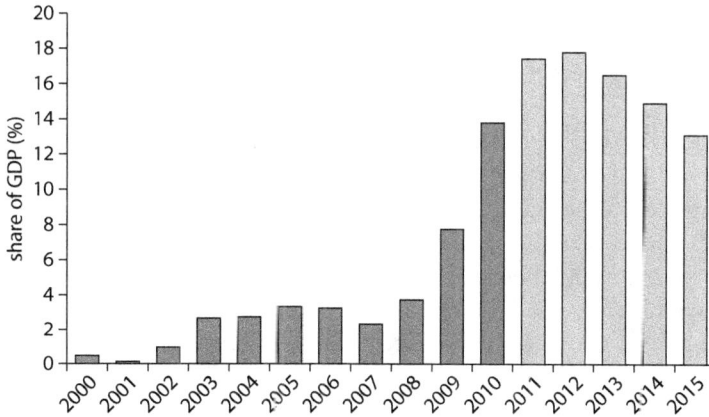

Source: Background paper, IV.1.

agreement with the Catholic Church and other religious organizations to deliver social services. As part of this agreement, these organizations charge school fees in exchange for managing and delivering social services. In public-private partnerships, the regulator monitors the quality of services delivered and the fee structure, while relegating management to a private operator. The principle of public-private partnerships is also being applied to road management, with the government in partnership with local companies, but success to date has been mixed.

Priority Setting for the New Government

The new government that will take office following the elections in November 2011 will be expected to formulate an economic program. It will have the opportunity to adopt an economic emergency action plan that could boost economic growth and accelerate employment opportunities for skilled workers. The parameters for such a plan are already being identified in the second-generation Poverty Reduction Strategy Paper that is being developed using a participatory approach. It is clear that no single action plan can solve the development puzzle of a large, diverse, and complicated country like the Democratic Republic of Congo. All actions have financial, political, or institutional costs, so there is an urgent need to prioritize and sequence the reforms.

This study proposes that the new government consider applying the lessons learned from tangible successes to boost state effectiveness, infrastructure, and private sector development. Successes and failures with four instruments provide the basis for the analysis: coordination among those who control or influence policy, application of new technologies, leveraging of external anchors, and development of social accountability networks.

Policy coordination among those who control or influence policy is the most effective instrument but also the most challenging. The report and background studies identify cases in which elites have jointly agreed on policies and implemented them effectively—for example, adoption of the 2006 constitution; the opening of major transport arteries such as the RN4, which connects Kisangani to Uganda; and acceptance of the 2002 decree, which allows only four agencies to be present at the border. Each of these three examples has its downside: the 2006 constitution provides legitimacy, but not state effectiveness; the transport arteries levy "road maintenance fees" that are not used for this purpose; and a diagnostic trade integration study published by the government documents the presence of a multitude of agencies at the border. Sustained implementation of agreements that build trust by delivering consistent, reliable public services is still not realized in the Democratic Republic of Congo.

Technologies and external anchors are both effective when fully operational but require national support to get started. We consider three examples in which modern technology has been used to deliver services successfully: (a) employment of a biometric survey in the security forces, (b) the expansion of automatic teller machines into smaller cities, and (c) mobile telephones. Each of these cases began at a time when the country or sector was in disarray. Reforms proceeded largely in the absence of a national partner in the case of telecommunications and in the presence of strong assistance from external partners in the case of security. Each of these reforms could be applied to similar cases, but either have not been implemented or have been implemented with long delays. A biometric census has not yet been conducted in the education sector, reform in the electricity sector is slow at best, and mobile banking services are unlikely to be delivered by end-2011 (although the governor of the central bank and the minister of telecommunications have agreed on regulatory issues). It appears that technology can play an important role in promoting broad-based development, but only if it is, at least initially, actively supported by domestic partners and strong collective agreements at the political economy level.

The role of domestic partners is even more important for the use of external legal and institutional anchors. This report looks at three inspiring successes: (1) the Democratic Republic of Congo's engagement with the United Nations and the Bretton Woods institutions, (2) the China framework agreement for infrastructure development, and (3) the absence of exchange controls that allow widespread use of the U.S. dollar. The first two are based on the initiative of the Congolese authorities. The circulation of U.S. dollar cash transactions does not require support from the authorities, but the national government has accepted dollar-denominated bank accounts, loans, and other financial contracts as a means of assuring financial stability. The importance of national support is also evidenced by the important cases that remain unresolved: (a) enforcement of arrest warrants by international courts, (b) the attraction of a foreign partner to manage the water utility Regideso, and (c) enforcement of external dispute settlement panels. These cases remain unresolved either because the authorities have not implemented agreements that parties agreed to voluntarily or because foreign investors fear that the authorities will fail to implement agreements in the future.

In principle social networks are the most efficient and effective means of assuring government accountability. Social networks empower users to hold service providers accountable. Historically, this stakeholder concept has remained undeveloped in the Democratic Republic of Congo, and even today the examples that we have identified are more conjectural than detailed case studies. The 2006 elections were free and fair, but reports indicate that since then elected politicians have had only limited contact with their constituents. Farmers and rural communities depend on rural roads, which continue to function, thanks to social networks that monitor maintenance. By contrast, urban roads barely function, even though road maintenance would more than compensate for the total cost of damage to cars.

Social accountability appears to be developing at the local level, while remaining well below par at the national level. The impact of local success stories is illustrated most vividly by the impact of peace and stability on agricultural development. As recently as 2008, agricultural productivity was low in conflict-affected provinces such as North and South Kivu; in a conflict-affected environment the time horizon is too short for investment in agriculture. However, improvements in security have allowed renewed private investment. The exact terms for such improvements are beyond the scope of this report, but arrangements that are rooted in local conditions may have a better chance of success than arrangements that are externally imposed. Such bottom-up growth is important and explains the poverty alleviation achieved in recent years.

In addition to bottom-up reforms to boost agriculture, the authorities have used some innovative policy instruments. Score cards advise parents on the performance of teachers and school administrators, and the farmers who use rural roads maintain them collectively.

Coalitions among those exercising or influencing power in the Democratic Republic of Congo have played a crucial role in initiating or unleashing key reforms. However, some of these reforms have floundered because such coalitions are difficult to maintain over time. In practice, technology, external anchors, or social accountability were effective in sustaining the reforms initiated by Congolese authorities.

This report finds interdependency in reforms that increase state effectiveness, expand infrastructure, and support private sector development. This interdependency goes beyond a virtuous circle in which better infrastructure contributes to private sector development and a stronger state, which could make more resources available for the construction of further infrastructure. In some cases, additional infrastructure does not strengthen private sector development or state authority. Similarly, some sectors are dominated by a single producer that influences state policy, illustrating that some firms are too large to be controlled by public policy. Policy makers may want to use an economic cost-benefit analysis to evaluate the impact of alternative policies and investments.

Managing Political Consolidation and Sustaining Growth

This report identifies several difficult realities confronting the enabling environment for inclusive and sustained growth. The risk that the country will return to a period of political instability and conflict continues to stifle growth, notably in agriculture. While large companies, including in the mining sector, have brought some wealth, this has by no means been broad based. Lagging reforms, including in the state-owned enterprise sector, have mounting economic and social costs.

The Democratic Republic of Congo's protracted conflict has left significant scars of physical destruction. A core challenge of the ongoing reconstruction is to reestablish infrastructure that is critical for growth and equity. New infrastructure will also need to be prioritized and responsive to opportunities for regional integration, as well as to changing population patterns, including population growth and urbanization. But as the experience of other countries demonstrates, developing the right "soft infrastructure" will be just as critical for longer-term prosperity as developing the right hard infrastructure. This begins with the ability to maintain and productively use the emerging base of infrastructure. Whether in transport or power, an adequate enabling environment will need to be in place to provide consumers and industry with competitive, but above all reliable, access to services.

Reforms in the Democratic Republic of Congo will take time. More than the formal "stroke of the pen" reforms, what matters to economic agents are the de facto and often informal realities of the business environment. These will condition what investments are made, and in which sectors, and will determine the overall prospects for growth and diversification. While growth has shown some signs of rebounding, it is starting from an extremely low base and is narrow, especially with respect to broader job creation. Increasingly, those with the power to influence and implement policy will need to demonstrate a credible commitment to building key parts of the country's soft infrastructure. While hard infrastructure may in the short term open the path to growth, soft infrastructure, such as adequate governance and institutions, is needed to sustain it.

Notes

1. The last census was conducted in 1984. According to official projections, the current population is 67 million.
2. The last systematic household survey—the 1-2-3 Household Survey—was conducted in 2005. A new survey is anticipated.

CHAPTER 1

Introduction

The Democratic Republic of Congo is a large country, with massive natural resources and an impoverished population (see table 1.1). With a total surface area of 234 million hectares, it is now the largest country in Sub-Saharan Africa.[1] After Brazil it has the largest rain forests in the world and 80 million hectares of arable land. Historically it was among the largest producers of copper, cobalt, and gold, but after years of neglect and a lack of exploration, known reserves are modest relative to their potential size. Today the Congolese population is estimated to be around 67 million, projected to reach 85 million by 2020. Despite its natural resources and agricultural potential, population growth is concentrated in the cities. An estimated 37 percent of the population, or 25 million inhabitants, is living in urban areas; by 2025, an estimated 40 million Congolese will be urban dwellers. Nationwide, 71 percent of the population lives below the poverty line, and poverty affects rural areas (about three-quarters) even more than urban areas (below two-thirds).

The Democratic Republic of Congo has had a turbulent colonial and postcolonial history. Independence in June 1960 was followed by the declaration of independence of the Kasai and Katanga provinces. Patrice Lumumba, the first elected prime minister, requested support from the Soviet Union. After only 10 weeks, he was deposed in a coup d'état,

**Table 1.1   Poverty Indicators in the Democratic Republic of Congo
and Sub-Saharan Africa, 2007**

percent

Indicator	Congo, Dem. Rep.	Sub-Saharan Africa
Poverty rate	71.3	—
Gross school enrollment	85	—
Population with access to drinking water	22	55
Population with access to electricity	<10	24

Source: World Bank 2009.
— Not available.

deported, and assassinated in Katanga. General Mobutu Sese Seko suppressed the independence movement in the two provinces with the help
of foreign troops and officially became the head of the country in 1965.
From the beginning of his autocratic reign, Mobutu nationalized mineral
resources and created state-owned enterprises with monopoly rights
over the mining concessions. In 1970 he launched a 10-year plan (Goal
80), designed to transform the Democratic Republic of Congo into an
industrial country financed through domestic and external loans.
"Zaïrianization," an economic indigenization and nationalization cam-
paign, began shortly afterward. Thirteen months later, a "radicalization"
program was put in place to correct Zaïrianization, leading to even
greater concentration of interests and ownership in well-connected
hands. Zaïrianization and radicalization severely weakened the economy
(Meditz and Merril 1994), bringing inflation and unemployment, liqui-
dation of inventories and assets, and shortages of basic commodities,
scaring away domestic and foreign investors, and leading to massive
capital flight. The plantation economy virtually disappeared.

During the 1970s and 1980s, external shocks and influences led to
economic collapse in the 1990s. During the years of the cold war, the
country was a strategic ally of the United States against communist-
supported Angola. The economic situation became much more fragile
when the price of copper collapsed abruptly in the 1970s, after many
years of rapid growth. In 1986 the price of cobalt plunged 58 percent.
During the late 1980s mining output contracted sharply, triggering an
overall economic collapse. The central bank went bankrupt, and debt
stopped being honored as foreign currency reserves dried up; international players lost interest in supporting the country.

During the early 1990s the Democratic Republic of Congo descended
into a major war with dramatic humanitarian consequences. In the 1990s,

internal pressures led Mobutu to declare the Third Republic and promulgated a constitutional change that was supposed to pave the way for
democratization of the country. The looting of Kinshasa by the army in
1991–93 and Mobutu's inability to keep public services functioning further
weakened his government. War in neighboring countries to the east spilled
over to the Congolese territory. In 1997 Mobutu fell from power, and
Laurent-Desiré Kabila became the new head of the country, renamed the
Democratic Republic of Congo. This coup was followed by war, often
referred to as Africa's First World War, which, according to some estimates
caused up to 5 million deaths.[2] Per capita income in 2000 was less than a
third of that in 1970. Laurent-Desiré Kabila was assassinated in 2001, and
his son, Joseph Kabila, succeeded him as head of the country. The signing
of the Global and All-Inclusive Peace Agreement of 2002 triggered a
gradual restoration of peace. In 2006 the first democratic and multiparty
elections were organized, and Joseph Kabila was voted into office. Following
the peace agreement, battle-related deaths fell dramatically (see figure 1.1),
from a high of 50,000 in 1998 to a low of less than 500 in 2008.

Armed conflict continues in the eastern part of the country, increasingly concentrated in the Kivu provinces (see map 1.1). This conflict
continues with an ebb and flow of intensity rooted in competing interests,
not only over mineral resources but also over issues such as land and
citizenship. The government's efforts to impose the rule of law and secure
these eastern provinces have been thwarted by influential members of
the national army (United Nations 2009; Global Witness 2009), various
rebel groups preying on the local population, and the commercial traf-
ficking and, above all, exploitation of minerals. Measures taken to enforce
security in the east include the rapprochement with Rwanda in late 2008,
the joint operations of the Democratic Republic of Congo and Rwanda
against rebel groups (the Democratic Liberation Forces of Rwanda,
FDLR), the integration of the National Congress for the Defense of the
People (a Congolese rebel group) into the national army in March 2009,
and a government ban on mining in the eastern provinces. However, the
FDLR still controls about 30 percent of illegal mining in South Kivu
(Global Witness 2009).

The troubled history of the country has led to a scarcity of data, which
constrains policy and decision making (see table 1.2). The last census was
conducted in 1984, and there is no precise information on the size of the
Congolese population. This situation complicates not only economic
policy making but also core state functions such as the organization of
elections. Estimates of economic activity vary widely. The business

Figure 1.1   Long-Term Economic and Security Indicators

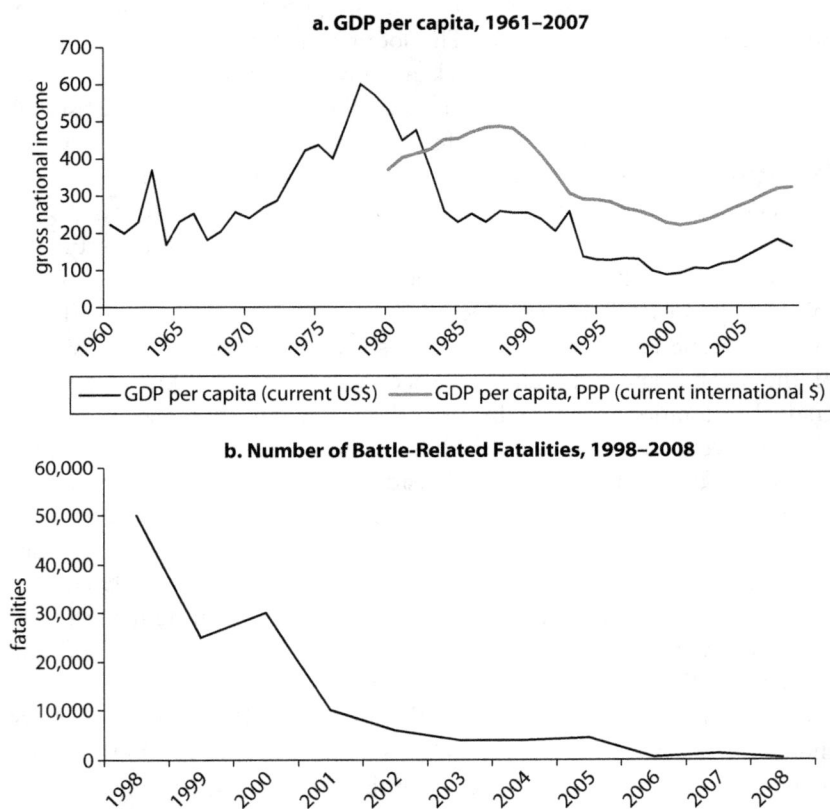

a. GDP per capita, 1961–2007

GDP per capita (current US$) ———— GDP per capita, PPP (current international $)

b. Number of Battle-Related Fatalities, 1998–2008

Source: World Bank 2010b.

Note: The shaded area in panel a indicates the period covered in panel b.

environment is known to be difficult, but information on opportunities for reform is not systematically available. In the Democratic Republic of Congo, competing priorities as well as the high costs of gathering and producing relevant information have been major impediments to documentation. The eagerness of the government and its development partners for precise data and analysis gave rise to an effort to compile a database of information on economic development in each of the provinces and to conduct a new Investment Climate Assessment Survey, which updated the 2006 survey.

The World Bank Group and the Congolese authorities are engaged in a major effort of data collection and analysis intended to inform the policy

Map 1.1   Geographic Location of Violent Events, 2006–08

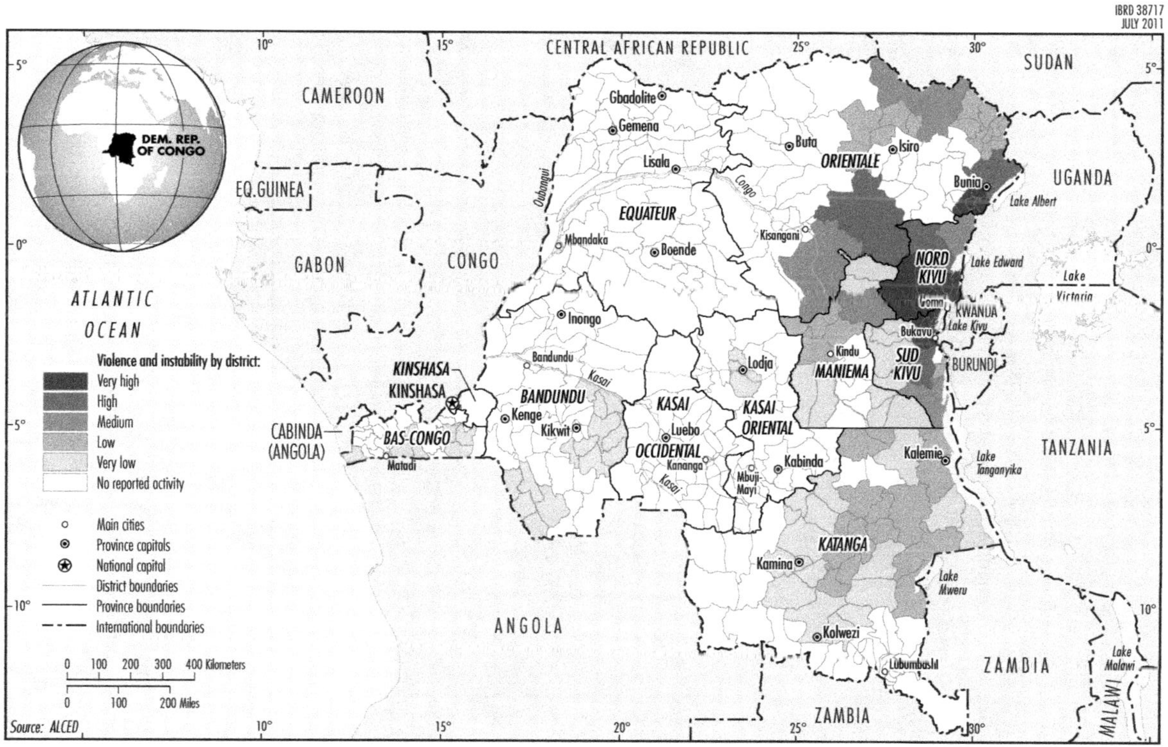

Source: Armed Conflict Location and Event Data, "ACLED Report on the Democratic Republic of Congo," Aug.–Sept. 2008, http://acleddata.com/documents/DRC%20Report%202.pdf.

Table 1.2   Select Historical Events in the Democratic Republic of Congo, 1960–2011

Date	Event
1960, June 30	The country achieves independence.
1965	Joseph Mobutu seizes power in a military coup.
1971	Country is renamed Zaire.
1973–74	Foreign-owned firms are nationalized.
1989	The country defaults on foreign loans.
1991 and 1993	Unpaid soldiers loot Kinshasa.
1993–97	Limited economic and political reforms are undertaken.
1997	Alliance of Democratic Forces for the Liberation of Congo-Zaire rebels capture Kinshasa, the country is renamed the Democratic Republic of Congo, Laurent-Desiré Kabila becomes president.
1998	Civil and international war ensues; Angola, Central African Republic, Namibia, Rwanda, Uganda, and Zimbabwe all intervene.
1999	The Lusaka Ceasefire Agreement is signed.
2000	The United Nations Security Council authorizes peacekeepers, known under their French acronym MONUC.
2001	President Joseph Kabila takes office upon the assassination of his father, reengaging with the International Monetary Fund, the World Bank, and other traditional partners.
2002	The Global and All-Inclusive Peace Agreement is signed.
2003	An interim constitution is adopted, and foreign troops withdraw from the country.
2005–06	A new constitution is adopted by referendum; a democratically elected president and Parliament take office.
2006–08	The constitution is promulgated; insecurity continues in North Kivu, a US$9 billion resources-for-infrastructure agreement is signed with China.
Late 2008, early 2009	A financial and security crisis takes place; emergency support is sought from traditional creditors and bilateral diplomatic relations with Rwanda.
2010	US$12.3 billion in debt relief is received under the Heavily Indebted Poor Countries Initiative and the Multilateral Debt Relief Initiative.
2011	Electoral and other procedures are revised in an amendment to the constitution.

Source: Authors.

debate. Initiated in 2008, this analysis is focused on identifying a potential trajectory leading to economic growth and human development. Fourteen background studies were commissioned, which tackle cross-cutting impediments to economic growth, analysis of sector-specific performance, the status and trends of trade and private sector development, as well as the macroeconomic environment. These studies were compiled in the four volumes that are synthesized in this document (see box 1.1).

Box 1.1

Main Points of the Background Papers

- *Institutional dynamics.* The 2006 constitution is only partially implemented. A coalition government is expected to remain the norm and needs to become adept at formulating policy. A more technocratic approach to public policy implementation requires civil service reform and decentralization of government services.
- *Macroeconomic policy constraints.* The stabilization of the economy and the resumption of growth have strengthened the political efforts to achieve a peace agreement. Challenges remain in fiscal policy; in particular, efforts are needed to enhance the contribution of the mining sector to the economy.
- *Growth diagnostics.* The main obstacles to agricultural development are security and public safety, infrastructure, and access to finance. For nonagricultural activities the main obstacles are access to finance, lack of electricity, and government failures.
- *Economic growth as an instrument for poverty alleviation.* Security and stability are the main obstacles to inclusive economic growth that could alleviate poverty.
- *Agriculture.* Of all sectors, agriculture has the highest potential for alleviating poverty through employment growth and its impact on food prices.
- *Natural resource management.* Artisanal mining and illegal logging activities employ hundreds of thousands of people at low wages; the formal sector employs few people and creates impressive value added. The most important potential contribution of the formal sector is the generation of fiscal revenue; backward and forward linkages are shallow.
- *Urban issues.* Rapid population growth and limited rural opportunities are fueling one of the most rapid processes of urbanization in Africa. The main challenges are urban planning and, in particular, land use issues.
- *Construction.* The rapid expansion of infrastructure investment is fueling demand for construction services, but the sector is ill prepared to satisfy that demand after a dearth of activities in past decades. Public policy could encourage specialization and the development of skills.
- *Infrastructure.* The need for investment in the power, transport, and telecommunications sectors is daunting, but service delivery could also be improved at modest cost by making management more efficient.

(Continued next page)

Box 1.1 *(continued)*

- *Human capital and labor markets.* Labor productivity is low or stagnant, and the education system is not equipped to address the labor market demands.
- *Private sector development.* New data document the poor state of the investment climate to the detriment of small and medium-size companies. Some large well-connected companies may have benefited from the investment climate.
- *National trade policy and trade facilitation procedures.* The Democratic Republic of Congo's national trade policy is similar to that of its peers, but trade facilitation procedures are slower and more costly. The underlying reason is that each agency wants to collect its own fees. The authorities plan to introduce a single window that will collect all fees.
- *Regional integration in the Great Lakes region.* Important opportunities for regional integration exist in the Great Lakes region. However, abusive authorities discourage the activities of small traders.
- *Regional integration in the western corridor.* Trade within the Greater Kinshasa–Brazzaville metropolis remains divided along national borders. Pressures for change are growing and likely to increase further as the Pointe Noire–Brazzaville corridor develops; the port of Matadi remains congested.

This analysis of the potential trajectory for the Democratic Republic of Congo is grounded in the country's institutional environment and its current economic performance. The background studies focused on clarifying the objectives of Congolese economic policy and the environment in which policy is formulated and executed. The studies assess the impact of policies, particularly on the poor. They present the areas in which the authorities have decided to focus their efforts and discuss the factors that may determine the effectiveness of policy in these areas.

The research conducted for this study focused on the specific context of the country, applying international methods. Applied growth analysis has evolved to recognize the importance of country context in defining well-prioritized and feasible growth strategies (see box 1.2). Five features condition how the Democratic Republic of Congo will work to achieve sustained growth. First, the country has among the worst development indicators in the region. Second, it scores quite low on a range of international governance indicators. Third, it shares vast borders with nine countries, with significantly different levels of economic activity and

Box 1.2

Recent Developments in the Economic Growth Literature

Approaches to applied economic growth analysis have shifted from presumptive (or normative) to diagnostic (Rodrick 2008). Rather than emphasizing a list of comprehensive reforms, greater emphasis is now placed on identifying a set of priority areas and actions to promote and sustain growth. According to Pritchett (2008, 19), a growth diagnostic process "should lead to a set of recommendations for a limited number of concrete actions that are country-specific and feasible (administratively and politically) which are likely to promote favorable growth outcomes." While methodologies may differ, the general thrust of this evolution has been to prioritize and arrive at more feasible policy interventions at the country level in support of the growth agenda.

Effective governance and political economy are vital ingredients in a country's growth agenda. The Commission on Growth and Development (2008) underscores the importance of leadership and effective government for implementing successful growth strategies. Underlying the requisite characteristics of capable, credible, and committed government are broader issues of governance and political economy. Particularly in the realm of helping to implement effective growth strategies in developing countries, international development partners have increasingly sought to gain a better contextual understanding of these issues (Fritz, Kaiser, and Levy 2009; Levy and Fukuyama 2010).

regional integration. Fourth, it is blessed with significant natural resources, such as subsoil assets and forestry. Finally, it remains a conflict-affected country. This final feature has obvious humanitarian implications and continues to undermine the general rule of law. In addition, it is likely to condition the priorities of the government and the decisions that economic agents make with regard to investment and commerce.

The audience for this study is Congolese policy makers and their supporters. This analysis aims to help policy makers to prioritize their interventions and unlock a virtuous cycle of growth and poverty alleviation. The premise is that a lack of information and understanding of the impact of alternative policies has prevented the coalition building that is necessary for successful policy formulation and implementation. The Democratic Republic of Congo has a fragile but stabilizing macroeconomic environment. Critical institutional reforms are lagging, and elements of political culture and general capacity issues create a downside risk for the economy. Coalitions can be formed only with a clear vision of the rewards and the allocation of those rewards among the partners. Sustaining those coalitions requires confidence-building measures to ensure that rewards are allocated as agreed.

The study provides a snapshot of the country's current economic performance, a detailed analysis of cross-cutting constraints to growth, and an understanding of the levers needed to support an economic rebound. Using new analytical data, chapter 2 describes the country's growth performance. The study focuses on three areas of constraints and potential levers to boost economic growth: government effectiveness (chapter 3), infrastructure development (chapter 4), and private sector development (chapter 5). Chapter 3 relates generally to security and public safety and more broadly to macroeconomic outcomes and governance indicators. Authorities and donors alike have identified infrastructure as a priority, but there are differences of opinion as to which infrastructure priorities are the most urgent and how these can or should be financed. Similarly, there is a consensus that the private sector should be the main engine of growth, fulfilling its natural role in economic development, and several instruments are being implemented to unshackle private sector growth. Chapters 4 and 5 therefore explore the key constraints in these areas and analyze the prioritization of investments, reforms, and instruments for implementation. Chapter 6 draws lessons from the successes and failures of efforts using four instruments to advance economic reforms: (a) coalitions among those who execute and influence policy, (b) technology, (c) external institutional anchors, and (d) social accountability networks.

Notes

1. After the independence of South Sudan.
2. According to the International Rescue Committee, the number of excess deaths in the Democratic Republic of Congo since 1998 is 5.4 million, of which 4.6 million occurred in the five insecure eastern provinces (IRC 2007, 18). The Human Security Report Project (2010) challenges these estimates, contending that the total number of casualties is only a third of the IRC estimate. Needless to say, armed violence has had an enormous impact on the civilian population. In turn, its economic implications, very much the subject of this report, have been equally significant, with the Congolese economy contracting up to 15 percent of GDP a year as a result of violence in the late 1990s (Koyame and Clark 2002).

CHAPTER 2

A Fragile Renaissance

The country remains fragile in the wake of a war that cost millions of lives during 1996–2002.[1] The war was itself the result of a rapid descent from relative prosperity during 1960–80 that was based on commodity exports and therefore deflated when commodity prices collapsed in the 1980s. Poor development sapped the potential of the mining sector, and corporate and public institutions were too weak to absorb the shock; policies became unsustainable. Unpaid soldiers ransacked Kinshasa in 1991–93, and the city has not yet recovered. Infrastructure collapsed, and today only four provincial capitals out of 10 can be reached by road from the national capital and province of Kinshasa. Data concerning growth and the Millennium Development Goals have, in some cases, begun to rebound, but the country continues to suffer from more than a generation of lost development. Per capita income is only back to its 1994 level, about half the high point of the early 1970s. Potential economic growth is high, but so is mortality.

Stability, inflows of sovereign capital, and positive terms of trade are critical ingredients that affect the macroeconomic performance of the Democratic Republic of Congo. The country's natural resources, through exports of copper, cobalt, gold, and diamonds, provide for an influx of rents with some linkages to other sectors. However, the country's dependence on these resources continues to make it highly vulnerable. Sustaining a virtuous development trajectory, which leverages the potential wealth from mining, forests, and hydropower, will require both longer-term perspectives and supportive, capable institutions. The risk that the Democratic Republic of Congo will lurch back into conflict remains real, as is the risk that economic development will remain shallow and narrow at its base. The government must therefore take credible measures to invigorate long-term private investments, while ensuring that economic growth is inclusive and benefits all of the country's citizens.

This chapter describes the main features of economic development since the mid-1990s and ends with a discussion of policy outcomes. Development since the end of the conflict has been confined to specific geographic areas, such as the main cities and mining regions; there has been no physical or institutional capacity to reach every region of the country. Government authority is gradually being restored; technical control over macroeconomic policy was established first, and now other policy areas are being developed. This chapter provides details on macroeconomic performance, the status of poverty, regional disparities, the coexistence of integrated and isolated sectors, economic risks, and the impact of governance.

A Growing, but Weak, Economy

Economic growth since the end of the war has not yet restored the Democratic Republic of Congo to its previous prosperity. From 1988 to 2001, GDP declined every year other than 1995. The war contributed to this decline, but the fall in GDP started earlier (see figure 2.1). Economic mismanagement triggered a vicious cycle of erratic fiscal and monetary policies, loss of hard currency through a decline in export receipts, financial meltdown, and hyperinflation. This cycle, in turn, led to a virtual halt in private and public investment. Economic conditions continued to deteriorate during the war. After the war ended in 2002, economic growth averaged some 5.8 percent a year, about 3 percent per capita. By 2007, after five years of growth, the economy had returned to prewar (1994) levels, but the population was by then almost 50 percent larger than in 1994. The postconflict bounce was not as strong as in other Sub-Saharan African countries (Background paper, II.3). In 2008 the Democratic Republic of Congo was still one of the poorest

Figure 2.1   Economic Growth, 1960–2010

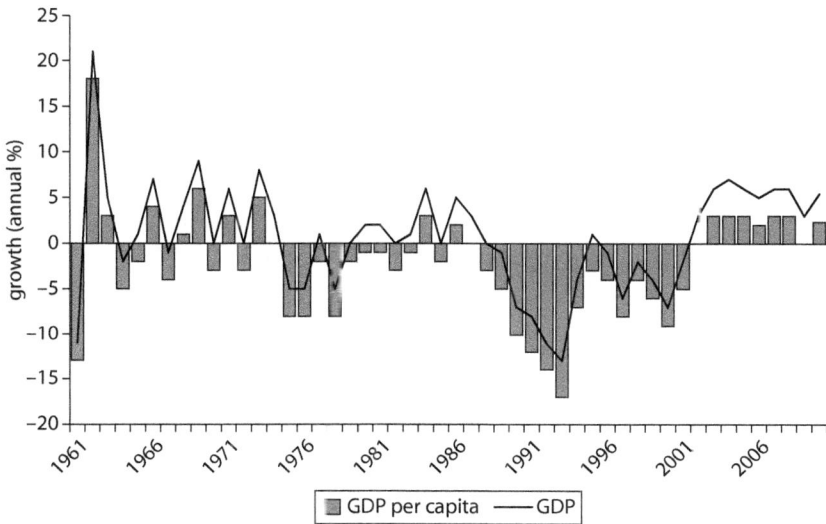

Source: Background paper, II.2.

countries in the world, with GDP per capita of US$95 (in 2000 terms), US$0.25 a day.

The performance of different sectors has varied enormously in recent decades. Conflicts have played a major role in the fluctuation of GDP, but a separate analysis of the causes of the variations in sector performance provides an understanding of the structure of growth over time.

The mining sector declined and recovered ahead of other sectors. The nationalization of the mining sector was led by the creation of Gécamines in 1966, followed in the 1960s and early 1970s by the nationalization of all mining companies. In the 1980s and 1990s, Gécamines alone represented 60 percent of national exports, and the mining sector as a whole represented 80 percent, generating 50 percent of government revenues. Between 1988 and 1995, copper production dropped a staggering 90 percent, from 470,000 tons to a mere 34,000 tons. Zinc and cobalt production nearly ceased. Manganese production stopped in 1975. As the economy opened up in the context of the 2001–03 economic reform, mining prices started to recover on international markets, and international investors were keen to reinvest in known mineral deposits. During 2001–05 the mining sector accounted for about a third of all growth (see figure 2.2).

Figure 2.2 GDP Growth, by Sector, 1996–2010

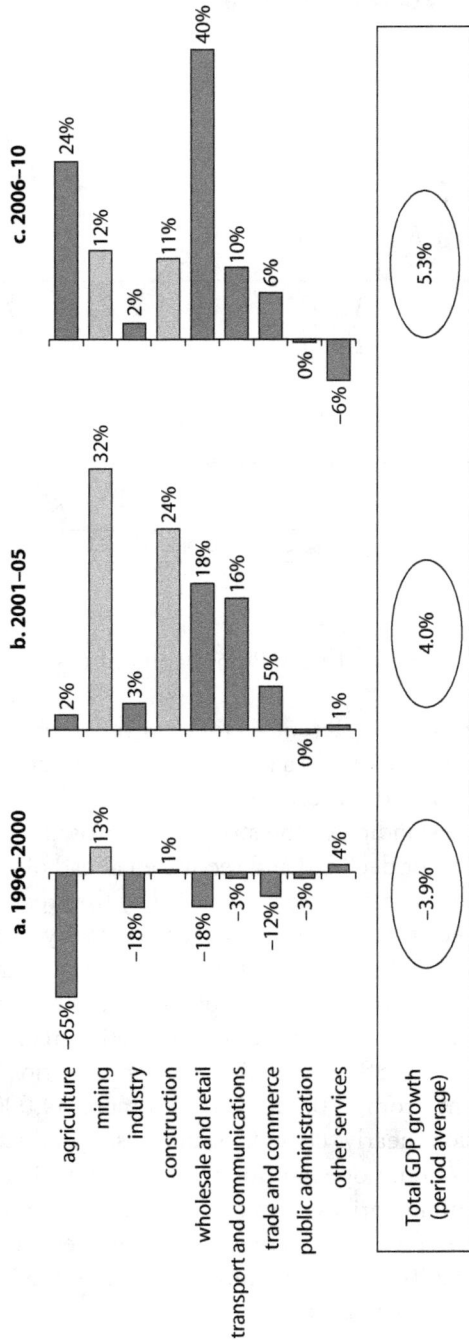

Source: Background paper, II.2.

"Zaïrianization" during the 1970s undermined the viability of large-scale agricultural projects and disrupted the maintenance of rural infrastructure and support services. The collapse of infrastructure and mass displacement of the population, due to the lack of security, further contributed to the decline in agriculture during the war. Rehabilitation of rural infrastructure, notably roads, started in 2001–05 and contributed to the agricultural recovery that took hold during 2006–10. Data collected at the level of the provinces suggest that this recovery is stronger than reported by the central bank data.

The dynamics of urban development changed as a result of the war and agricultural collapse. The transformation of urban areas started dramatically with the looting of Kinshasa by the Congolese army who were protesting unpaid wages during 1991–93. Reduced opportunities in the agriculture sectors led to a massive migration of the population to urban areas; most of these migrants engaged in informal trade because legitimate jobs were scarce.

The construction sector, which had practically disappeared during the war, has been growing since 2000 in response to rising demand. Starting from a low base, the sector reached some 9 percent of GDP in 2010. Donor-funded projects and rising public investment have contributed a large part of this growth. The sector suffers from a lack of qualified personnel, partly because few relevant skills are being transferred from foreign-owned companies to local suppliers, and growth of the construction sector has slowed to just above average GDP growth.

Improved Economic Growth and Modest Poverty Reduction

The Democratic Republic of Congo remains one of the poorest countries in Africa despite the recent improvements. The poverty rate is estimated to be 71 percent. Some 80 percent of households report not being able to meet their basic needs, and the human development index is well below the average for Sub-Saharan African countries (see table 2.1). Nevertheless, there has been improvement in some indicators; the infant mortality rate is estimated to have fallen from 126 deaths per 1,000 live births in 2001 to 89 in 2008, while the maternal mortality rate fell from 1,289 deaths per 100,000 births to 944 during the same period. Poverty is greater in rural than in urban areas, with 35 percent falling in the poverty trap in rural areas compared to 26 percent in urban areas.[2] The probability of being poor is higher among households whose members are working in the agricultural sector.

Table 2.1   Human Development Indicators in the Democratic Republic of Congo and Sub-Saharan Africa, 1980–2010

Year	Congo, Dem. Rep. Human development index	2000 = 100	Sub-Saharan Africa Human development index	2000 = 100
1980	0.267	132.8	0.293	93.0
1990	0.261	129.9	0.306	97.1
2000	0.201	100.0	0.315	100.0
2005	0.223	110.9	0.366	116.2
2006	0.227	112.9	0.372	118.1
2007	0.235	116.9	0.377	119.7
2008	0.231	114.9	0.379	120.3
2009	0.233	115.9	0.384	121.9
2010	0.239	118.9	0.389	123.5

Source: http://hdr.undp.org/en/countries/.

Gross primary school enrollment rates increased from some 64 percent in 2006 to more than 80 percent in 2008. According to the latest evaluation report for the Poverty Reduction Strategy Paper and the Heavily Indebted Poor Countries (HIPC) Initiative, education represented more than 10 percent of the government's poverty-related expenditures during 2006–08. Expenditures in education have grown faster than expenditures in the health sector, and spending on education is now comparable to that of investments in infrastructure. Nevertheless, the high cost of both health and education limits access by the poor, and a disconnect remains between services delivered and the large needs of the population in general and larger families in particular. Challenges remain, as the efficiency of the system still lags behind the African average. Between 4 million and 5 million school-age children are still out of the system. Educational attainment in primary education is only 14 percent, according to the 2010 Multiple Indicator Cluster Survey, which also indicated that 42 percent of Congolese children ages 5 to 14 is involved in child labor.

Women are particularly affected by poverty. School enrollment is lower for girls than for boys. Only 28 percent of women receive a salary. The average income of a woman in paid employment is about half that of a man, which is much lower than in Uganda (69 percent), Burundi (77 percent), or Rwanda (79 percent). Women are more vulnerable to the human immunodeficiency virus/acquired immunodeficiency syndrome, and some 1 to 3 percent of women reportedly have been raped in the Democratic Republic of Congo.

The persistence of poverty can be understood in the context of rapid population growth, modest investment, and inefficient use of existing resources. The country has a young population, and the labor force is increasing rapidly. During 2001–10, the labor force expanded much faster than the capital stock (see table 2.2). The population is also growing some 2.9 percent a year, one of the highest rates worldwide. The Congolese population numbers some 67 million. Further, investment has been limited to the mining regions and Kinshasa; in Kinshasa more than two-thirds of the workforce is considered unemployed or underemployed (Background paper, III.3). Postconflict provinces have attracted practically no new investment; for example, South Kivu has received only 1 percent of the value of all investment projects approved by the National Investment Promotion Agency, while the workforce has expanded some 2–3 percent a year.

As noted, data collected at the provincial level suggest that agriculture may be growing faster than reported by the central bank, offering prospects for poverty alleviation. The data collected in the provinces on agricultural production are the most reliable (see table 2.3). A substantial upward revision in agricultural growth would explain the modest, but significant, decline in poverty indicators. Agriculture affects poverty directly through employment and indirectly through lower food prices.

Natural Resource Disparities and Regional Inequality

Regional inequality has reemerged as a major issue. In 2010 the three richest provinces (Bas Congo, Katanga, and Kinshasa) accounted for 34 percent of the population, but generated more than 55 percent of GDP (see map 2.1). The two poorest provinces, Kasai Occidental and Maniema, accounted for 10 percent of the population, but only 4 percent of GDP.

Table 2.2   Sources of Economic Growth (Adjusting for Human Capital), 1992–2010
percent

Indicator	1992–95	1996–2000	2001–05	2006–10
Real GDP growth	−6.8	−3.9	4.3	5.3
Factor accumulation	2.8	−0.7	4.1	4.3
Labor	6.0	0.4	6.9	5.8
Capital	−2.0	−2.4	0.0	2.0
Total factor productivity	−9.6	−3.2	0.2	1.0

Source: Background paper, II.2.

Table 2.3   Real Growth in Agricultural Production, by Province, 2007–10
percent

Province	2007	2008	2009	2010	Average, 2006–10
Bandundu	9.4	3.9	0.2	1.3	3.7
Bas Congo	14.0	17.2	8.3	10.1	12.3
Equateur	5.6	5.0	18.4	5.0	8.3
Kasai Occidental	14.5	8.0	9.6	6.7	9.7
Kasai Oriental	6.6	8.2	1.7	13.6	7.4
Katanga	−22.7	12.8	5.7	5.9	−0.6
Kinshasa	63.8	17.2	14.8	12.0	25.3
Maniema	0.3	3.9	18.2	13.6	8.7
North Kivu[a]	−3.9	−1.8	3.2	8.2	1.3
Province Orientale	2.0	4.8	8.3	6.8	5.5
South Kivu[a]	−23.7	−8.9	3.1	12.0	−5.3
Average 11 provinces	−0.6	6.7	7.0	7.7	5.2
National average reported by the central bank	3.3	3.0	3.0	3.0	3.1

Source: Central bank and provincial authorities.
a. Provinces experiencing conflict during 2006–09.

The mining sector accounts for some 12 percent of GDP, but its economic impact is much larger. In addition to the value added captured in the GDP statistics, mining provinces also benefit by supplying services and inputs to the mining sector and by processing mining products. In some provinces, mining revenues are also the cause for and the means of financing conflict. On balance, mining resources have an ambiguous impact on economic development.

The mining sector in Katanga contributed more than 50 percent to GDP in 2010, and the contribution to growth during 2006–10 was even larger.[3] Multiplier effects may have raised the contribution of mining to economic growth to more than 90 percent. Katanga's poverty rate is slightly above the national average, but inequalities still exist between the population working in mining and those working in other sectors.

In contrast, the mineral riches of the eastern provinces have played an important role in continuing armed conflict at the expense of economic development. Despite its potential resources, Kivu is one of the poorest provinces, with a poverty rate of 85 percent. South Kivu also has a high rate of gender discrimination regarding access to education; less than 2 percent of women ages 15 to 49 have completed a secondary education.

The national capital Kinshasa benefits from international transfers and taxes that are administered by the national government on behalf of the

Map 2.1   Per Capita Income and Average Annual Economic Growth, by Province, 2006–10

2010 US$ and percent growth per year, average 2006–10

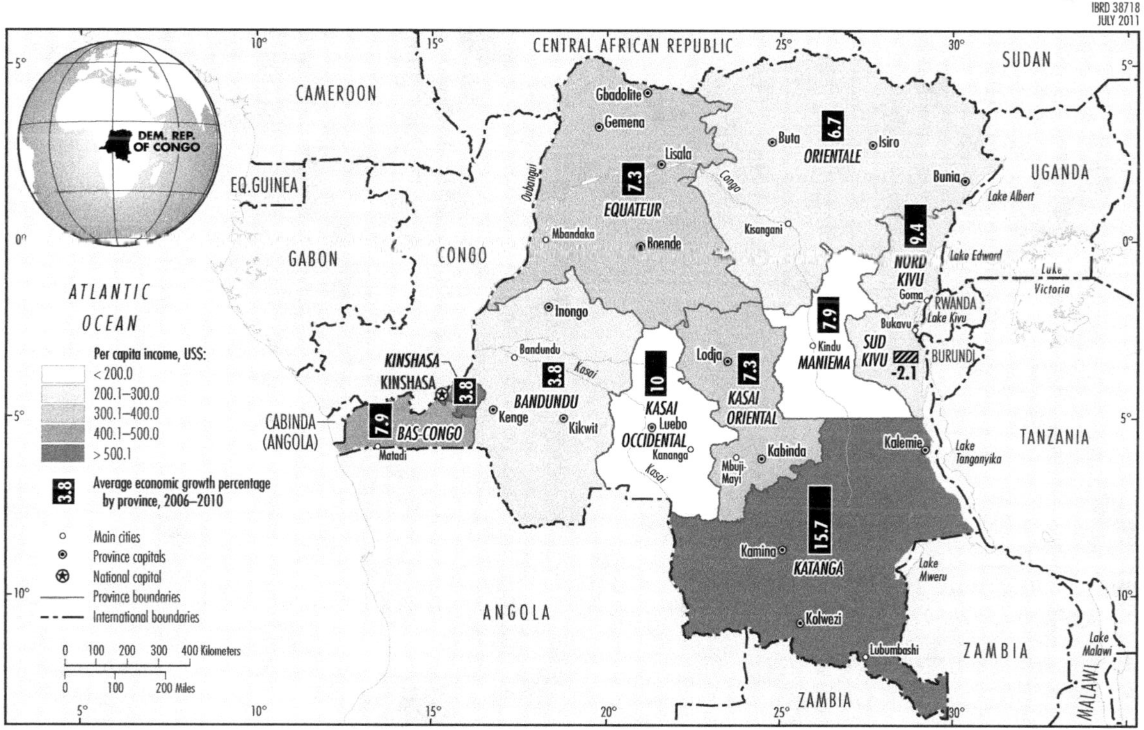

IBRD 38718
JULY 2011

SUDAN

UGANDA

CENTRAL AFRICAN REPUBLIC

CAMEROON

EQ. GUINEA

GABON

CONGO

ATLANTIC OCEAN

DEM. REP. OF CONGO

CABINDA (ANGOLA)

ANGOLA

ZAMBIA

TANZANIA

MALAWI

RWANDA

BURUNDI

Lake Victoria

Lake Albert

Lake Edward

Lake Kivu

Lake Tanganyika

Lake Mweru

Lake Malawi

ORIENTALE — 6.7

Bunia

Isiro

Buta

Kisangani

NORD KIVU — 9.4

Goma

SUD KIVU — -2.1

Bukavu

MANIEMA — 7.9

Kindu

EQUATEUR — 7.3

Gbadolite

Gemena

Lisala

Bwende

Mbandaka

KASAI ORIENTAL — 7.3

Lodja

Kabinda

Mbuji Mayi

KASAI OCCIDENTAL — 10

Lueba

Kananga

Kcosi

KATANGA — 15.7

Kalemie

Kamina

Kolwezi

Lubumbashi

BANDUNDU — 3.8

Inongo

Bandundu

Kenge

Kikwit

Kcosi

KINSHASA — 3.8

Kinshasa

BAS-CONGO — 7.9

Matadi

Per capita income, US$:
- < 200.0
- 200.1–300.0
- 300.1–400.0
- 400.1–500.0
- > 500.1

Average economic growth percentage by province, 2006–2010

3.8

- Main cities
- Province capitals
- National capital
- Province boundaries
- International boundaries

0   100   200   300   400 Kilometers

0   100   200 Miles

Source: World Bank estimates.

31

provinces. Kinshasa accounts for almost half of national merchandise imports but generates less than 1 percent of exports.[4] Natural resources, produced in the rest of the provinces, are consumed indirectly by imports of goods in the capital city.

"Trade facilitation" charges are levied upon entry to and exit from the territory, benefiting Bas Congo, Katanga, and to a lesser extent South Kivu, where these charges are levied. The Diagnostic Trade Integration Study (Government of the Democratic Republic of Congo 2010a) estimates these fees at some US$120 million a year (about 1 percent of GDP), but the total impact, including multiplier effects, may be much larger.

The conflict-affected provinces have not systematically benefited from transfers from richer provinces. In 2010 estimates of refunds from the national government to provincial treasuries ranged from CGF 1,700 per capita in Kinshasa, one of the richest provinces, to CGF 5,500 per capita in Maniema, one of the poorest. However, the second-largest transfers were to Bas Congo, one of the richest provinces, while the second-lowest transfers were to Bandundu, one of the poorest. An infrastructure fund envisaged in the constitution may lead to more equality, but it is not yet operational.

Coexistence of Integrated and Isolated Sectors

At the macroeconomic level, the Congolese economy is well integrated with the world economy. Following years of rapid growth, exports plus imports of goods and nonfactor services had reached 140 percent of GDP by 2010 (figure 2.3). Inflows of foreign direct investment (FDI) declined after 2008 but remain well over 5 percent of GDP. As FDI declined, gross foreign aid disbursements picked up, exceeding 5 percent of GDP in 2009–10. These gross percentages of foreign aid disbursed exclude HIPC debt relief, which freed up resources as debt service obligations declined.[5] Foreign aid was initially focused on humanitarian relief but is shifting toward development projects (see box 2.1).

Certain parts of the economy are well integrated with international markets:

- Mining output is almost completely designated for international markets. When international demand falls, as in late 2008 and early 2009, this sector contracts, with dire consequences for suppliers.[6]
- The border regions in the Kivu provinces as well as Katanga are well integrated with international markets, thanks to a lively cross-border trade and available road or rail infrastructure. In the Kivu provinces,

Figure 2.3   Investment, Aid, and Trade, 2000–10

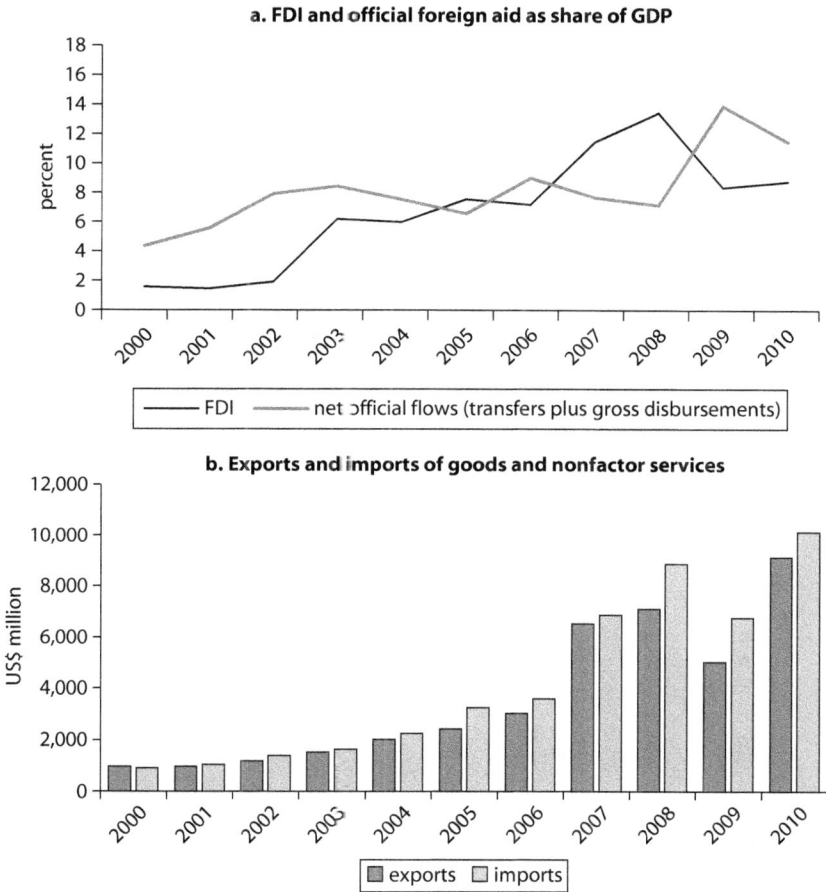

a. FDI and official foreign aid as share of GDP

FDI ⸻⸻ net official flows (transfers plus gross disbursements)

b. Exports and imports of goods and nonfactor services

■ exports □ imports

Sources: Central bank and International Monetary Fund.

small traders, who cross the border more than once a day, are largely responsible for these exchanges. In Katanga such trade is affiliated with the mining sector. By contrast, the equally important opportunities for cross-border trade in the Kinshasa-Brazzaville region are largely unexploited.

- The war-ravaged eastern provinces and Kinshasa benefit from foreign assistance. The amount of aid is modest in other parts of the country.

The concentration of investment, trade, and aid in specific provinces reflects the transport infrastructure. Only four provincial capitals are

Box 2.1

Foreign Aid, by Donor, Sector, and Region

The reengagement of international partners in 2001–02 involved rescheduling of arrears at concessional terms, the largest bilateral creditors being the United States and France. The United States remained one of the most important partners up to the elections in 2006 but has since then been overtaken by the United Kingdom and multilateral agencies such as the International Development Association and the African Development Bank.

The composition of aid also has changed over time. Initially humanitarian aid was important and continues to constitute almost 50 percent of total aid flows in the conflict-affected eastern provinces. However, social services, such as education and health, are a larger share of total aid flows. In response to the financial crisis in 2008–09, donors provided general program assistance on a one-off basis. Assistance to production-oriented sectors such as agriculture remains modest, but various bilateral donors, including Belgium and the Republic of Korea, plan to expand their activities in this area (see figure B2.1).

Figure B2.1   Foreign Aid, by Creditor and Sector, 2006–09

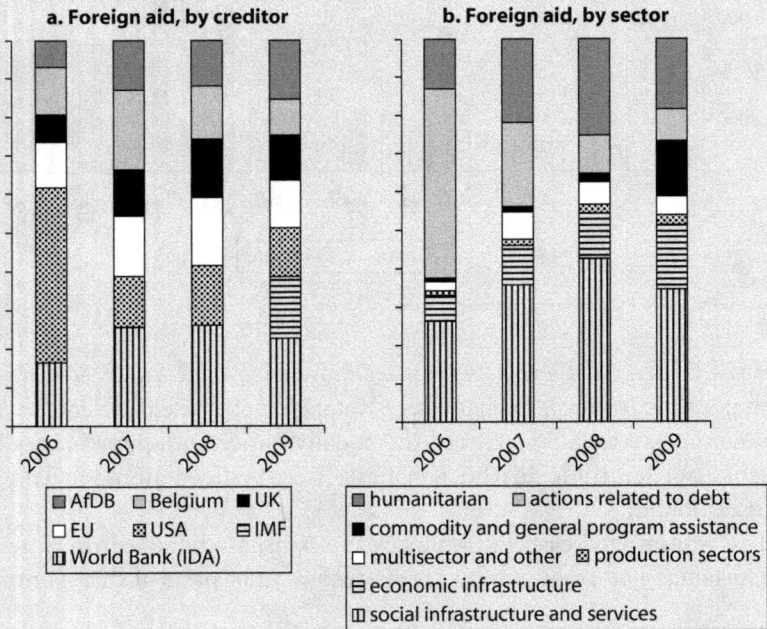

a. Foreign aid, by creditor

b. Foreign aid, by sector

■ AfDB   □ Belgium   ■ UK
□ EU   ⊠ USA   ⊟ IMF
⊞ World Bank (IDA)

▨ humanitarian   □ actions related to debt
■ commodity and general program assistance
□ multisector and other   ⊠ production sectors
⊟ economic infrastructure
⊞ social infrastructure and services

Source: OECD data.

accessible by road from Kinshasa. The Congo River and its Kasai and Ubangi tributaries form a natural transport system but can only be used during daylight due to the poor marking of danger points. An air transport system exists but has a poor safety record and is used sparingly by foreign businesses and officials. Only 10 percent of roads are in reasonable or good condition, and the railroad system barely functions, depriving the country of vital components of a multimodel transport system. Transport systems that have been refurbished such as the RN4, which connects Kisangani to Uganda, have had a large impact on economic growth, trade, and investment.

Communication technologies are growing rapidly, but availability remains limited. A competitively priced mobile phone system exists, and this system uses modern technology provided by foreign owners of partners in the mobile telephone companies. However, in the absence of broadband Internet, connections are slow and unreliable, and the economic benefits of telecom services are limited (Background paper, IV.1).

Most of the country's population and territory is isolated from global markets, operating in autarky

- Subsistence agriculture generates some 40 percent of GDP, engaging about 60 percent of the workforce. Linkages with urban and international markets are limited as a result of poor infrastructure; lack of security, especially in the eastern provinces; high fees; and harassment, particularly at international borders.
- Even people in urban areas are isolated. Public transport is costly, if available, and telecommunications are difficult in the absence of electricity.
- Limited skills are a barrier to labor mobility. Workers who receive on-site training in rural construction tend to move to urban areas afterward. However, the opportunities for such training are rare, and most people do not move.

Improved Macroeconomic Indicators, but High Risks

Macroeconomic policy has improved, but risks remain high. Inflation has fluctuated wildly during the last decade, declining from more than 500 percent in 2001 to reach single digits before rising to more than 40 percent in 2009 and then returning to single digits in 2010 (see figure 2.4). Reflecting the dollarization of the economy, wide swings in inflation have been matched by exchange rate movements. External

Figure 2.4   Government Balance, Net Credit to the Government, and Inflation

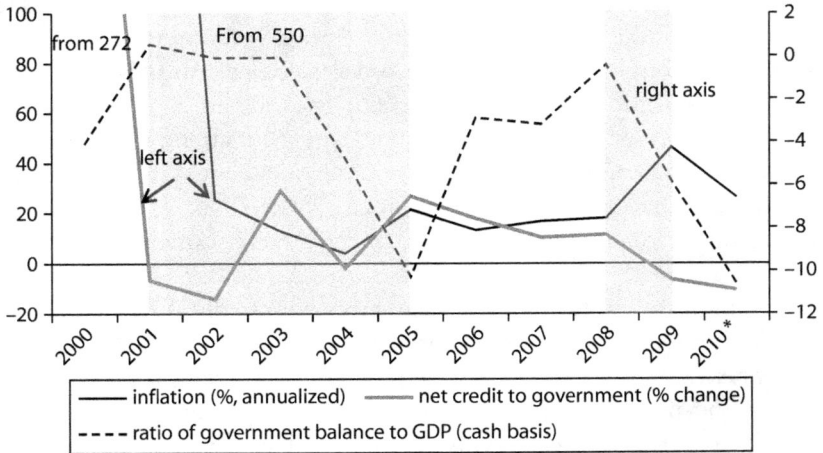

Source: Background paper, II.2.

public debt declined to under 50 percent, down from over 120 percent, thanks to debt relief under the HIPC Initiative and the Multilateral Debt Relief Initiative (MDRI) in 2010,[7] but has been trending up again since then. Four main risks are threatening the country's fragile macroeconomic stability:

- Fiscal balance is maintained on a cash basis, but not on a commitment basis (see table 2.4). Such policies can be justified as emergency measures, but their continued use over sustained periods of time undermines the credibility of fiscal policy.
- Concerns about security affect the composition of spending. In 2010 the defense budget was fully executed, while the education budget was 25 percent underexecuted, with even lower rates for other ministries.
- There is no formal deposit insurance scheme, but failures in banking supervision pose a fiscal risk as bank deposits tend to be implicitly guaranteed by the fiscal agent.
- The Democratic Republic of Congo remains at risk of debt distress. Following HIPC and MDRI debt relief, new debts have been contracted and the ratio of debt to GDP is rising, despite rapid GDP growth. The authorities have accumulated new loans from (a) the International Monetary Fund, as part of its US$550 million Extended Credit Facility arrangement; (b) the infrastructure package of the joint Democratic Republic of Congo and China agreement, which includes loans with

Table 2.4 Fiscal Balance on a Commitment and Cash Basis, 2001–10
% of GDP

Year	Fiscal balance	
	Commitment basis	*Cash basis*
2001	−1.7	2.0
2002	0.5	0.8
2003	−5.2	−1.0
2004	−4.3	−0.8
2005	−3.9	−5.9
2006	−0.6	1.3
2007	−3.5	1.2
2008	−3.3	0.7
2009	−4.2	0.3
2010	2.4	3.4

Source: Congolese authorities and World Bank staff estimates.

a grant element of some 47 percent;[8] and (c) project loans from nontraditional creditors such as China and India, which have a minimum grant element of 35 percent each. The main risk is that activities funded with the new loans will not contribute to growth and exports sufficiently to free up resources for debt service.

Lack of Good Governance and the Functioning of Economic Activities and Public Services

International indicators suggest that governance in the Democratic Republic of Congo continues to be an area of elevated concern. The country ranks close to the bottom of governance indicators for Sub-Saharan Africa. There may have been a slight improvement during 2000–09, but underlying indicators remain volatile, and the country's overall ranking compared to its peers has not improved. Almost all governance indicators improved during 2002–05 as the country emerged from the conflict, only to decline again in 2008–09 (see figure 2.5). Renewed emphasis on governance is a critical element of the country's upcoming projects to spur growth and improve the business climate.

- The Democratic Republic of Congo's rising fiscal revenues are mobilized at high cost; small companies make informal payments amounting to more than 3 percent of their revenues (Background paper, IV.3). Taxes

Figure 2.5   Governance Indicators, 2000–09

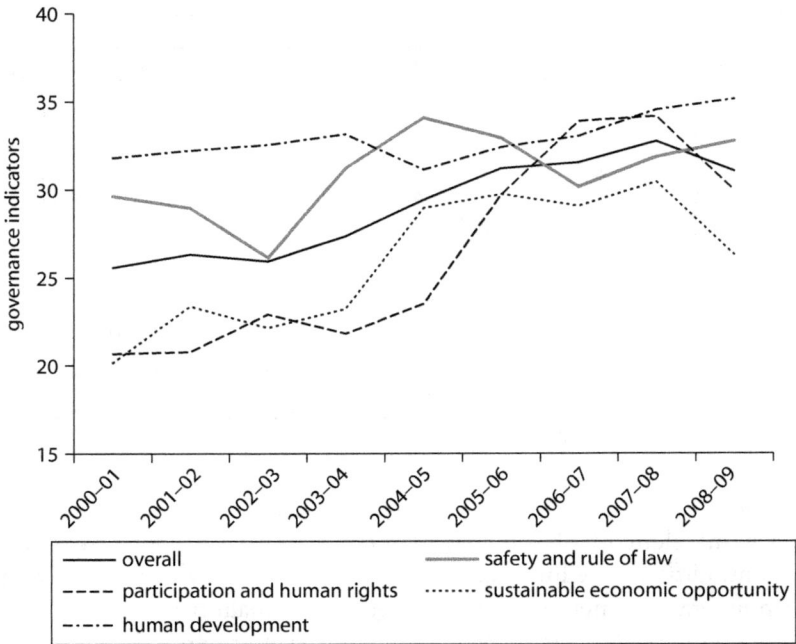

Source: Mo-Ibrahim Foundation.

imposed on large companies cannot be challenged in a cost-effective manner.
- Poor oversight undermines the quality of government expenditures. The 2010 Public Procurement Law has not yet been implemented, although it is legally in force, creating uncertainty for public contractors. The budgeting of debt-financed infrastructure does not follow criteria that can be objectively monitored and hence may pose a risk to external sustainability (Background paper, II.2).
- A lack of protection for individuals against violence undermines the allocation of resources and the efficiency of the population's efforts. For example, human rights abuses of small traders who operate legitimate businesses in the Kivu provinces undermine their efforts to make a living (Background paper, V.3).

Poor governance has a large impact on all companies, but the nature of the impact may vary depending on the size of the company. Small and medium-size companies are forced to pay a much larger share of sales in

Figure 2.6   Percent Enrollment in Primary and Secondary Education, 1984–2007

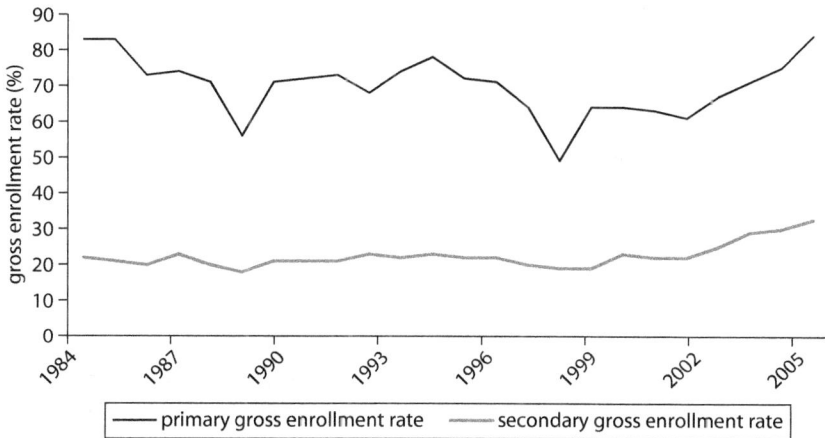

Sources: Background paper, IV.3.

the form of informal tax payments than larger companies (Background paper, IV.3). This burden on small companies slows their growth rate substantially. By contrast, large telecommunications and mining companies are challenged by the tax and regulatory authorities in a more formal manner that also raises the cost of doing business. In practice, some of the large companies have been able to deal with these challenges and have continued to prosper.

Services delivered by state-owned enterprises have deteriorated over time; for example, the state-owned electricity supplier (National Society for Electricity, SNEL) serves less than 10 percent of the population, and access to potable water delivered by the state-owned supplier (Regideso) has gradually declined. In contrast, services delivered in partnership with religious organizations, nongovernmental organizations (NGOs), and foreign partners have gradually improved; since the end of the war, the share of the population with access to health care and education has gradually increased (see figure 2.6). Financial contributions from households (parents, in the case of education) have played a crucial role in financing these gains. Services provided by NGOs, religious organizations, and foreign donors, although reliable, remain costly, partly because government officials benefit from the service fees (World Bank 2008).

The impact of poor governance has also varied by regions. Transport and regulatory costs on the Kinshasa-Matadi corridor have translated into higher prices for consumers. In contrast, cross-border transactions by

small traders have reduced the costs for consumers in the eastern provinces. Similarly, trade policy measures may have stimulated import sub-
stitution activities by mining companies to a much larger extent in
Katanga than in other provinces.

Priorities to Improve Economic Outcomes

The Congolese economy has improved since 2003: large companies
and recently agriculture have grown rapidly, but small and medium-size
companies have grown modestly. During 2006–10, aggregate economic
growth in the provinces, led by agriculture, was double the rate reported
in the national statistics compiled by the central bank. This development
was driven by suppliers to local markets, benefiting the poorest among
others. During the same period formally registered companies employed
in the range of 1.2 percent of the workforce. Assuming the total workforce is some 24 million people, this amounts to 300,000 jobs.[9] A limited
number of large companies continue to prosper. These differences in
employment growth are known as the "missing middle." Although the
missing middle is evident in many countries, the almost complete absence
of employment growth in the middle—the pattern in the Democratic
Republic of Congo—is an outlier.

Despite this progress, the Congolese population still suffers from poverty, and regional inequalities remain high. The Democratic Republic of
Congo's positive economic growth starts from a very low level, and the
poverty rate remains one of the highest in the world, affecting both urban
and rural areas. Access to basic services is limited, child labor affects
42 percent of children from ages 5 to 14, and woman are especially
vulnerable to various forms of poverty and violence. There has been an
economic rebound in specific regions, including mineral-rich Katanga,
and in the capital city of Kinshasa. However, wealth is not distributed
equally throughout the country, and the poorest provinces, such as
Bandundu, receive among the lowest transfers.

Macroeconomic and governance indicators are improving, but they
remain areas of concern. Security still affects the composition of the
Congolese budget; the threat of violence and instability in the east influences budget execution, which prioritizes defense expenditures over
social and infrastructure expenditures. HIPC debt relief in 2010 may
have improved the country's access to some publicly supported export
credit agencies. It is important that the activities, financed through newly
contracted loans, contribute sufficiently to acceleration of growth as a

means to sustain external debt. Governance remains a cross-cutting issue, affecting economic performance, entrepreneurs, and the delivery of basic services to the population.

These policy outcomes point to three common themes that are discussed in subsequent chapters: (1) inability of the state to implement economic policies effectively, (2) lack of infrastructure to exercise policy across such a large country, and (3) obstacles to private sector development.

The following chapters present both challenges and avenues of progress to address the three main obstacles to achieving broad-based economic growth in the Democratic Republic of Congo. The challenges presented include government effectiveness (chapter 3), infrastructure (chapter 4), and development of the private sector (chapter 5). Government effectiveness is linked to security and public safety, but also more broadly to macroeconomic outcomes and governance indicators. Infrastructure has been identified as a priority by authorities and donors alike, but there are differences of view on which infrastructure priorities are most urgent and how these can or should be financed. Similarly there is a consensus that the private sector should be the main engine of growth, fulfilling its natural role in economic development, but employment and business development still face major constraints.

Notes

1. This report focuses on the 2002 to 2010 period. It notes the critical juncture provided by the Global and All-Inclusive Peace Agreement of 2002, which effectively ended the war known as Africa's First World War. This is not to say that armed conflict ended. Organized violence continued in the east, such as Ituri in 2002–04 and the Kivu provinces from 2005 to the present. As the 2011 *World Development Report* notes, violence after the political settlement of war often increases, and while the data are poor, violence and the fear of violence clearly are continuing features of life in the Democratic Republic of Congo (World Bank 2011).

2. The poverty trap measures the severity of poverty and is defined by the average distance separating an individual's revenue from the poverty line.

3. Forestry resources play a similar role in Province Orientale and Equateur, but the benefits are much smaller. Even in these provinces, forestry contributes only some 2 percent of GDP.

4. Data on international exports of nonfactor services are not available by province.

5. Nominal HIPC and MDRI debt relief is equivalent to more than 100 percent of GDP, but the benefits accrue over time in the form of lower debt service payments and better access to credit markets.

6. In October 2008, 42 small and medium-size smelters closed as international copper prices fell below their operating cost of some US$4,000 per ton. The closure of these companies deprived an estimated 600,000 informal "artisanal" miners of an outlet for their produce and thus their livelihood.

7. In July 2010 the Democratic Republic of Congo obtained some US$12.5 billion in debt relief, including some US$7.5 billion from the Paris Club, leaving a total stock of some US$2.9 billion.

8. Following standard World Bank–IMF methodology (see Background Paper, II, 2).

9. The last systematic household survey—the 1-2-3 Household Survey—was conducted in 2005. A new survey is anticipated.

CHAPTER 3

Government Effectiveness

Many of the outcomes presented in chapter 2 are related to the government's inability to fulfill its role. In the Democratic Republic of Congo, the government has been only partially able to (a) protect the population from predation, (b) implement macroeconomic policies that allow the population to benefit from the country's natural wealth, and (c) establish a transparent public policy that would encourage the development of a market economy. Development during the past 15 years has been seriously lacking in the absence of a functioning government. Predation by armed groups, which began during the war, has continued, not just in the mines and eastern provinces This development has undermined effective public policy, since only the state is able to tax and reward legitimately from economic activities. Legitimacy is derived from political consensus based on transparency. The importance of transparency was recognized in the governance compact adopted by the first democratically elected government in 2007.

Steps to an Improved Political Consensus

Political fragmentation is rooted in the history of power dynamics. The main obstacle to the establishment of institutional capacity has been fragmentation of the elites who should be able to set policy and influence outcomes. This fragmentation goes back to policies adopted by President Mobutu (1965–97), who systematically undermined horizontal networks that could challenge his authority.[1] During the war (1996–2002) ethnic appeal and the resulting social fragmentation was used to fuel conflict at the local level. War ended in 2002, when disputes were settled through political agreements instead of violence.

From Peace Agreements to the New Constitution: An Evolving State Structure

The peace settlement of 2002 was based on the principle of power sharing between the president and four vice presidents (the 1+4 model). This model created an effective and expedient policy setting that facilitated a complex reform agenda and stimulated long-term economic growth. An interim constitution, also based on the power-sharing model, was put in place in 2003. The constitution was finalized in 2005 and adopted by referendum, and the first democratic elections in 40 years took place in 2006.

The 2006 constitution replaced the power-sharing interim constitution of 2003 with a president–prime minister model, checks and balances were introduced, and the constitution established that power would be shared between the central and subnational governments. Critical constitutional provisions were shielded from amendments that could drive a reconcentration of power. A complex legislative process was introduced, built on equivalent powers of the lower and upper chambers of Parliament. The volume of legislation adopted during 2007–10 was significantly smaller than during the transitional government because of this process.

The period 2006–10 was one of consolidation and stabilization, but not enough was done to render the government effective. The average tenure of national ministers was lengthened under the 2006 constitution, and the coalition appears poised to serve the full parliamentary period. However, the coalition did not articulate a shared strategic vision, and the Council of Ministers functions poorly. Also, the Parliament has adopted unrealistic budgets, and the announced policy priorities have not been implemented; the authorities are left with substantial discretionary power. The constitution created safeguards for such developments, principally by delegating major responsibilities to the provinces and providing them with independent fiscal resources.

Three critical reforms that were broadly agreed as necessary have suffered significant delays, highlighting the need for a stronger central government. These are the Procurement Code, the Public Finance Law, and adherence to the Organization for the Harmonization of Business Law in Africa Treaty.

Government effectiveness requires reaching a consensus on the objectives of government. Agreement among elites has been hobbled since the time of Mobutu, and this situation has persisted because of the intervening history of violence, external intervention, and sheer size of the country. Agreements are regularly broken, including the agreement to implement the budget as passed. The lack of strong public interest organizations reduces the capacity of citizens to hold elites accountable for their failure to represent the public interests. The current state of governance not only reduces the incentives for elites to protect the public interests, it also makes it difficult for them to make lasting agreements with each other.

Transition from Existing Security Arrangements
To address instability, security sector reform has been launched as part of the reconstruction and development process. Led by the United Nations Organization Mission in the Democratic Republic of Congo and the European Union (EU), backed by the EU Advisory and Assistance Mission for Security Reform in the Democratic Republic of Congo and the EU Police Mission for the Democratic Republic of Congo, and joined by donors such as France, Japan, South Africa, the United Kingdom, the United States, and others over time, the focus has been on three sectors: justice, the police, and the military. Civil liberties are violated with impunity throughout the country (Background paper, II.1). State authorities, in particular the military and police, participate in these violations, which highlights the lack of protection accorded to the population and the public interests. In recent years, the Democratic Republic of Congo has made some progress by addressing discrete sources of conflict, adopting the outline of a policy framework of security sector reform and a new Organic Law of Police, and recruiting new magistrates. Yet the country still faces instability, particularly in those areas where the culture does not support a public interest–oriented mind-set.

The lack of security is a fundamental constraint on economic growth. The state is associated with weak capacity, predatory behavior, and corruption. Investments favor some groups, regions, and sectors, without a general framework that fosters private investment and constructive relations with local communities. The private sector lacks the incentive to develop in line with long-term public interests and instead focuses on commerce and short-term gains. In local communities, poverty and violence fracture social capital and trust in the state; subsistence production is preferred over commercial production in an effort to avoid expropriation.

The Democratic Republic of Congo recognizes these challenges and wants to build on the success of the 2006 elections. The government has taken the following steps to address the massive challenges related to security and justice:

- From 2004 to 2010, more than 140,000 combatants were disarmed and demobilized.
- In 2009 the rapprochement with Rwanda led to joint military operations to address the continuing presence of foreign armed groups, notably the Democratic Liberation Forces of Rwanda, the Hutu rebel group.
- In 2009 the National Congress for the Defense of the People, the Congolese rebel group, was integrated into the national army.
- In 2010 virtually all mining activities were embargoed in the Kivu provinces and in Maniema, in an effort to deprive rebel groups of their income.
- In 2011 the embargo on mining activities in the Kivu provinces and Maniema was lifted.

Trust among the population and potential investors needs to be rebuilt. The government has made tentative steps to reform the armed forces (estimated at 140,000) and the police (90,000), but key issues remain regarding training, downsizing, and pensioning. Above and beyond the need to enforce the rule of law, key security priorities (such as rapid response and border control) are needed to encourage the engines of growth, such as agricultural production, the free flow of goods, and the mining sector. In turn, given the lack of trust in state structures and fiscal constraints, such sector reform will need to include greater oversight, transparency of the defense sector, and an improved system of public financial management.

Decentralization: A New Scheme for the State Structure

Decentralization was the central feature of the 2006 constitution, which envisioned a strongly devolved system of government, with autonomous provinces that have broad authority and responsibility. This new institutional system secured agreement from mutually distrusting political forces. The constitution foresaw a decentralized unitary state rather than a federal system and sought to prevent a reconcentration of power.

The constitution opened a new era for effective decentralization, with the following features, which have yet to be implemented:

- *Revenue sharing.* The constitution mandates that 40 percent of domestic revenue be allocated to the provinces and levied "at the source." There is some debate on the interpretation of "at the source"; for example, regarding export and import duties, does source relate to the location of collection or the location of production and use? The lack of resolution on this particular issue has important consequences for both the business environment and the country's infrastructure development program. Provincial governments, deprived of what they consider to be their constitutional entitlement to revenue, have started levying additional local taxes and fees, which puts an additional burden on private operators.

- *Transfer of competencies and staff to the provinces.* The constitution defines primary and secondary education, health, and agriculture and rural development as decentralized sectors; in other words, the management of service delivery is the responsibility of the provinces and local governments, but the standards are set at the national level. This principle is reflected in the Law on Provincial and Local Self-Government, adopted in 2008. As of end-2010, no competencies had been transferred, although interim regulations on public service management, applied since mid-2009, have effectively placed provincially-based staff under the authority of provincial ministers. Fragmented authority and accountability on staffing issues have fueled allegations of the misuse of wage bill funds (which make up more than 40 percent of expenditures), and while the extent of fraud is difficult to establish, it clearly has a negative impact on the provision of public services.

- *Design of decoupage.* Administrative territorial reform, or *decoupage*, is an unresolved issue. The constitution calls for splitting the current 11 provinces into 26; however, this division has not been implemented. Serious risks inherent in the premature implementation of this constitutional provision include the following: (1) ethnic tensions could be fueled in certain regions; (2) of the 26 new provinces to be created,[2] only four might be fiscally self-sufficient; and (3) a massive investment in administrative infrastructure is required, for which no funds are available. An amendment to the constitution adopted in early 2011 formalized the delay in implementing this provision.

- *Election of subprovincial authorities.* The constitution and the 2008 Law on Provincial and Local Self-Government provide for the creation of elected authorities at the self-governing level (the level of sectors, *chefferies, villes,* and *communes*); however, local elections have been repeatedly postponed. For the transition, the president has appointed all heads of districts and burgomasters. While (valid) logistical and financial reasons have been given for the repeated postponement of local elections, the absence of functioning local governments is a serious hindrance to the implementation of bottom-up economic development strategies.

Despite the institutional challenges, decentralization is likely to improve the accountability of provincial governments to their populations. The new arrangements have lengthened the average tenure of provincial governors, but they can still be removed by provincial assemblies as well as by the central government (Background paper, II.1, table 1). Governors who can deliver economic improvements or public services are less vulnerable to political removal. The population expects there to be a functioning public service that delivers services and creates jobs; there is an urgent need to resolve the challenges hindering the implementation of decentralization.

Civil Service Reform as a Necessary Step to Government Effectiveness

The government needs to deliver services and create an environment for growth, and this will require efficient internal organization. Today, serious issues are hindering the ability of the administration to provide adequate services. In addition to the limited monitoring and follow-up of the central government on policy implementation, the legal status of the public service is outdated, the number of staff employed is not known, the wage system is opaque, and the bulk of the public service workforce is nearing retirement; these are the main systemic constraints to organizational efficiency. Public service reform is a necessary step toward making government more effective and generating political will and trust among governing elites.

A complex civil service structure has been fueled by decades of crisis. The huge civil service networks throughout the country were built under the autocratic regime and have been largely dysfunctional since 1991. During and after the period of conflict, jobs offered to people in unstable situations were subsequently recognized, which made the civil service even more bloated and complex and added little to social stability. The public service wage bill is reportedly 40 percent of fiscal expenditure, but this includes only the officially registered and recognized civil servants. Today, five categories of people work for the civil service:

- Official civil servants who are registered and recognized (*régularisés* and *mécanisés*) in the system of the Ministry of Public Service and are paid a basic wage
- Official civil servants who are registered but not recognized (*non-régularisés* or *sous contrat*) in the system of the Ministry of Public Service and are not paid
- Official civil servants who are registered and recognized (*non-mecanises*) in the system of the Ministry of Public Service, but are not yet being paid
- New qualified recruits (*Nouvelles Unités immatriculées*) who are informally recruited civil servants who are registered in the system of the Ministry of Public Service and do not receive salaries but are paid standard "bonuses." These people have some qualifications to work in the public service but are not listed on the official payroll.
- New recruits without formal qualifications (*Nouvelles Unités non immatriculées*) who were added to the Ministry of Public Service to ensure social stability following the civil war. No data are available on their numbers, but they appear numerous in those provinces most affected by the war (the Kivu provinces and Katanga).

Several tentative civil service reforms were initiated in recent years, but no major achievements have been implemented. In 2003 the authorities launched a civil service reform with four objectives: (1) identifying the number of civil servants, (2) developing capacity for administrative management, (3) modernizing and improving human resource management, and (4) promoting good governance and professional ethics. The government decided to stop recruiting new employees in 2005 and to organize a manual census of public servants, with financing from South Africa. Despite this decision, recruitment mostly of *nouvelles unités* has continued, complicating efforts to complete the census.

In 2007 the government endeavored to simplify the salary structure for public servants.[3] In 2007–08, the government integrated allowances, traffic expenses, and housing allowances into the basic salary, reducing allowances to some 30–60 percent of total pay, down from 90–95 percent (with a reported average of 50 percent). However, allowances still exist in many ministries and continue to constitute an important part of remuneration. Allowances sometimes increase base salaries tenfold, even though the 1982 Law on the Status of Public Agents prohibits setting allowances at more than 66 percent of total salary. Allowances make civil servants more dependent on political patronage than they otherwise would be and contributes to the harassment of the private sector (chapter 5).

Retirement of civil servants is a major issue. Based on the 236,596 civil servants officially registered in the payroll system as of June 2010,[4] it is estimated that those having reached retirement age account for more than 60 percent of the entire public service (mandatory retirement criteria is 55 years of age or 30 years of service). While the legal obstacles that blocked the retirement process in 2005 have been removed, several issues remain:

• *Retirement pensions.* According to the law, civil servants on the official payroll are to receive indemnities composed of a repatriation fee and a retirement allowance calculated on base salary (excluding allowances); hence pensions may be significantly lower than final pay.
• *Access to the retirement package.* Approximately 25 percent of services are officially registered, and recognized civil servants are eligible for the retirement package. New recruits (*nouvelles unités*) are not eligible for benefits upon retirement.
• *Freed-up financial gains.* Wages constitute more than 40 percent of public expenditure, but cost savings from retirees may be offset by the need to recruit new employees to replace them.

Reforms require an understanding of the composition of human resources. Despite efforts to undertake a census since 2005, the Ministry of Public Service has faced logistical challenges, funding shortages, disagreements in government, challenges by *nouvelles unités,* and other political roadblocks. Still there are signs of progress; agreement was reached on a separate census of teachers that will be conducted after the general census of the public service. So far a census of teachers has been blocked by disagreements regarding methodology and the sharing of responsibility between the Ministry of Public Service and the Ministry of Primary and Secondary Education; teachers constitute 50 percent of all public servants. Sectoral ministries such as the Ministry of Environment and the Ministry of Defense have undertaken their own biometric census, which has identified a more precise number of officials. This due diligence eliminated "ghost officials" from the payroll and led to plans for restructuring the ministries: downsizing, hiring new civil servants, and retiring the retirement-age staff. While the Ministry of Public Service continues

to seek a harmonized census to identify the full scope of public administration, the biometric census undertaken at the provincial level, combined with a sectoral, vertical approach, may be a reasonable facsimile.

The State's Economic Challenges

The primary challenge to the Congolese state is to provide transparency
and accountability. However, addressing this challenge requires a modi-
cum of appropriate macroeconomic policies. Hence such policies are
discussed first.

Macroeconomic Discipline
Macroeconomic indicators improved quickly after the authorities
adopted appropriate policies in 2001. Inflation declined from some 500
percent in 2000 to single-digit levels in 2004, increased again in 2005
and 2009, but returned to single-digit levels in 2010. The decline in
inflation was related directly to responsible fiscal policy and a reduction
in the monetary financing of the budget. After some 12 years of continuous decline, economic growth turned positive, foreign direct investment flowed in, and international assistance increased. After three
public sector banks were liquidated in 2002, banking supervision
strengthened, but there are indications that it weakened again toward
the end of the decade.

The security and financial crisis of 2008–09 strengthened the authority of the president to maintain tight fiscal policies. The Congolese
economy remains largely dollarized, and gross foreign exchange reserves
provide a cushion in case of a crisis. During 2002–04 reserves doubled.
However, after that point, practically no reserves were accumulated; all
revenues above projections were spent. When copper prices dropped in
the wake of the international financial crisis in 2008, fiscal revenues
declined, and reserves were only US$27 million in early 2009. The
public sector received emergency support from the International
Monetary Fund (IMF), the World Bank, and others.[5] This dire situation
led to dramatic policy actions: a peace agreement with Rwanda was
reached, and domestic political forces realigned in early 2009; a bilateral loan agreement with China was amended to pave the way for debt
relief under the Heavily Indebted Poor Countries (HIPC) Initiative;
and fiscal policies were supported by an IMF program approved in
December 2009 (see figure 3.1).

Figure 3.1   Gross Foreign Assets in the Central and Commercial Banks, 2003–10

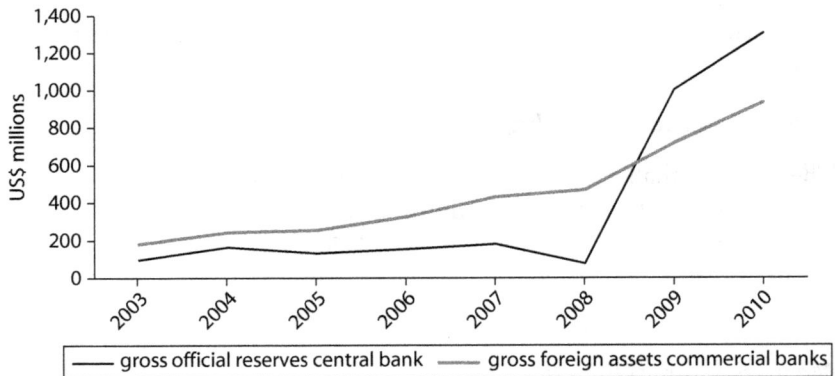

Sources: Central bank and International Monetary Fund.

Developments during 2002–10 demonstrate the challenges of implementing appropriate macroeconomic policies, including the following:

- Intersectoral and interministerial trade-offs require guidance from the highest political authorities and a consensus on policy objectives among all coalition parties.
- When policies are imposed from above, they are unlikely to be sustainable; when this happens, public investment suffers, and "retrocession" of revenues to the provinces leads to unpredictable outcomes that are not sustainable over time.
- Select public investment projects are moving forward under resources-for-infrastructure agreements, which have many positive elements, but are not subject to the same oversight that can be provided by a well-functioning system of public finance management.
- Banking supervision poses specific problems that go beyond mere technicalities as illustrated by the fact that some banks do not fully observe all prudential requirements.

Transparency and Accountability

Political uncertainty comes at high economic costs. Some uncertainty originates from market conditions and is to be expected in an emerging market economy (see chapter 5). However, in the Democratic Republic of Congo some policy uncertainty is willfully created. This principle applies at all levels; for example, the time needed to clear a container through customs ranges from one day to 10 weeks. Because the criteria on which this clearance is decided are unclear, private operators are likely to pay to get the container cleared in one day. By contrast, clear procedures for appeals and penalties for officials found to abuse their positions would reduce these officials' leverage. Transparency, accountability, and, in particular, social accountability are key instruments with which to address corruption.

The first democratically elected government introduced a governance compact upon taking office in 2007. The governance compact significantly improved transparency in a number of areas. As envisaged in this compact, the government would provide Parliament with transparent control over the state budget. However, increasingly the budget voted by Parliament is far larger than the available resources; their fundamental function of allocation of mobilized resources and regulatory oversight is not fully ensured; and, more generally, issues related to the management of public finances remain nontransparent (see box 3.1).

Information disclosure does not necessarily guarantee appropriate monitoring. In February 2008 the Court of Account revealed for the first time US$5 million worth of embezzlement cases in its audit report of

Box 3.1

Lack of Transparency in Public Finance Management

The Democratic Republic of Congo's public finance management system has to balance realistic revenue projections with Parliament-approved budgetary allocations and budget execution. Revenue agencies have an incentive to underestimate revenue targets: they receive 5 percent of the revenue they collect (10 percent for fines and penalties collected) up to the target revenue level, and 20 percent of revenues mobilized in excess of the target revenue level.

Parliament tends to overestimate budget revenues, as higher projected revenues allow a more generous allocation of resources. Budgets approved by Parliament do not affect the targets agreed to between the Ministry of Finance and revenue agencies.

Using the regular public finance procedures, the executive branch is constrained by the approved budget allocations. However, the executive branch has procedures for passing urgent expenditures. Expenditures approved under these procedures are retroactively integrated into the reporting system and not subject to budget ceilings approved by Parliament.

(continued next page)

Box 3.1 *(continued)*

During 2008–10, the approved budget for priority ministries and institutions increasingly exceeded the executed budget; the difference expanded to more than double the executed allocations. Within this wide envelope, the executive branch had full flexibility. Even so, urgent expenditures continued to be used and allowed the budget execution of the presidency and the prime minister's office to exceed their Parliament-approved allocation by 144 and 76 percent, respectively (see figure B3.1).

Figure B3.1   Budgets Allocated by Parliament and Budget Execution, 2008–10

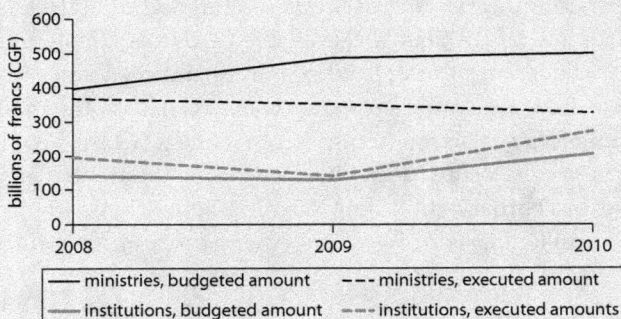

Sources: Ministry of Planning and staff calculations.

public expenditure for the period from December 2006 to February 2007. Despite a public outcry, notably from civil society, no arrests have been made. Similarly, the application of adopted legal texts is not monitored.[6] The Democratic Republic of Congo adopted 85 legal instruments in the period from 2003 to 2006, yet public agencies have apparently not been informed of or are willfully ignoring the new legislation. For example, Presidential Decree no. 036/2002 stipulates that only four agencies be represented at the border; the Diagnostic Trade Integration Study commissioned by the government documents the presence of a multitude of agencies active at the border (Government of the Democratic Republic of Congo 2010a).

Social cohesion can protect public interests but exists only in isolated cases. Private citizens have little capacity to shift government policy, and those individuals who do challenge the authorities are suppressed—as illustrated by the death of human rights activist Floribert Chebeya in 2010. Yet in Nande-dominated Butembo, key economic groups cooperated to improve the provision of public goods. Another success story is in Bas

Congo Province, where a donor tested the concept of road maintenance paid for by tolls collected by the community. These two cases demonstrate a form of social contract between the state (and elites) and the communities that enhances social cohesion and public interests at the same time.

Building on the Macroeconomic and Democratic Reforms: What Comes Next?

The Democratic Republic of Congo has made progress toward developing an institutional basis for effective government. It has adopted a revamped legal framework and modern institutional structure that has allowed it to implement sound macroeconomic policies supported by the IMF's Extended Credit Facility Program. The international community has recognized the most recent elections in 2006 as fair. To scale up and institutionalize these achievements, more needs to be done.

Government effectiveness requires a move toward coalitions that are willing to respect a more technocratic approach to policy making and service delivery. Such an approach requires agreement among coalition parties on economic policies that are publicly announced and whose implementation is verified. The discrepancy between announced policies and actual policy implementation undermines credibility and trust in public institutions.

The 2006 constitution envisages improving public accountability through decentralization. Decentralization is expected to make public policy more accountable and hence to improve public policy and raise state effectiveness. The obstacles to effective policy formulation and implementation at the provincial level range from a lack of financial and institutional resources, legal capacity, and security challenges to state authority in the eastern provinces. Despite these challenges, some provinces have made remarkable progress. For example, South Kivu is experimenting with participatory budgeting in which citizens are invited to express their budgetary priorities. Clarifying the national authorities' vision of public accountability at the decentralized level will be an important element of policy implementation.

Decentralization is a first step toward social accountability. The challenges of engaging with citizens will provide a powerful incentive for better formulation and implementation of policy. For example, parents paying school fees could challenge school administrators; contributors to road maintenance could question the delivery of road maintenance services; and civil society could have a role in monitoring security services.

Such monitoring would be even more effective if local officials were elected in a popular vote.

The state could also be more effective in its engagement with external partners. Following years of neglect, the Democratic Republic of Congo finds it difficult and costly to promote its interests in international arenas. It could learn from other countries, including large countries such as Brazil, which have effectively defended their interests in international legal forums. The key to success could be to centralize legal know-how in a single unit tasked with defending the country's interests in international forums. This would require a better-functioning central government and increased coordination among officials and the country's power structures.

Notes

1. In his first decade in power (1965–74), Mobutu embarked on a state modernization project. First, he shifted power and authority away from local authorities and toward Kinshasa. Second, he built up an administrative cadre to deliver services throughout the country, achieving 92 percent primary school enrollment. When copper prices plunged and oil prices soared in the mid-1970s, there were no longer resources to build support among the general public and to maintain the coalition among elites. The regime drew back from its service delivery strategy and relied instead on a two-pronged approach of using clientele payoffs to ensure the loyalty of key groups, while inhibiting the formation of coalitions among these groups, whether they were ethnic groups or different branches of the fragmented security services.

2. The plan was to create 21 provinces out of six existing provinces, while letting five others remain in their current set-up.

3. Public servants receive (a) salaries, (b) bonuses for performing specific tasks or working in certain locations and sectors, and (c) supplementary benefits for overtime work.

4. This number largely underrepresents the real size of the civil service today. The estimate can reach 1 million, including all *nouvelles unités*, security services, teachers, and doctors.

5. This need for emergency support is in contrast to the situation in the private banking sector. This sector was able to absorb the shock of the financial crisis without emergency support. The collapse of a commercial bank in late 2010 was not directly related to the financial crisis.

6. See no. 948/CAB/MIN/BUDGET/GHO/dj/2007 du 23 mai 2007 adressée au Président de la Cour des Comptes au sujet d'auditer les dépenses publiques de l'Etat du 1 Décembre 2006 au 28 Fevrier 2007.

CHAPTER 4

Unlocking the Infrastructure Challenge

Congolese infrastructure is in bad shape. Only four out of 10 provincial capitals are linked by road to the national capital, Kinshasa. Less than 10 percent of the population has access to electricity; although mobile phones are ubiquitous, the country does not have a national telecommunications backbone. Port costs are substantially higher, and delays are longer, than elsewhere. Rail transport is some 250 ton-kilometers, about a tenth of the volume during the 1980s. These infrastructure challenges have a major impact on economic development, private sector growth, and employment.

In the Democratic Republic of Congo the lack of infrastructure is not just an economic problem, it is a political challenge. The inability to travel by road across the country challenges the political unity of the state, and this issue is only gradually being addressed. President Kabila has visited all of the provinces to the extent possible by car, in some cases using newly opened roads. The construction of infrastructure is important to state building, but it is costly, and in some cases the use of alternative facilities, such as airports in neighboring countries, can achieve the same economic results.

Current Status of Major Infrastructure Sectors

This section focuses on power, transport, and telecommunications issues in the Democratic Republic of Congo. These three sectors are crucial for growth, employment, and some aspects of poverty alleviation. The following discussion excludes the important issues of water and sanitation as well as the delivery of health and education services. The latter are crucial if the country is to achieve the Millennium Development Goals, but they do not directly affect the country's economic growth and employment.

The Power Sector

Less than 10 percent of households have access to electricity in the Democratic Republic of Congo, one of the lowest rates in Africa. This low level of access is a major bottleneck to social and economic development. The power supply itself is unreliable, and those who have access to electricity experience frequent interruptions and an average of 10 days of power failure a month. These interruptions severely penalize private enterprises, which have to incur the additional cost of purchasing a back-up generator. New commercial connections to the network are frozen, forcing most commercial customers to rely on diesel generators.

Power generation is well within the country's potential capacity. The potential capacity for electricity production is estimated at about 100,000 megawatts from hydropower alone (the highest in Africa), but total installed capacity is approximately 2,400 megawatts, or less than 3 percent of that potential. Of this 2,400 megawatts, hydropower accounts for nearly 99 percent, with the remaining power being supplied by about 60 small and isolated solid-fuel thermal plants. A handful of large industrial enterprises maintain their own production capacity. The two hydropower plants at Inga account for 1,775 megawatts of installed capacity.[1] Despite the country's huge potential, domestic production is insufficient to meet the local demand and exports are limited. Only 48 percent of installed capacity is actually available.[2]

The transmission system in the Democratic Republic of Congo consists of several unconnected electricity networks (see map 4.1). Equipment is outdated, maintenance levels are insufficient, and new investment is minimal. The system does not have sufficient capacity to meet current demand. In particular, lines in the capital are overloaded, and the high-voltage direct current (HVDC) line between Inga and Katanga carries

Map 4.1 Electric Power Generation and Transmission System

IBRD 38719
JULY 2011

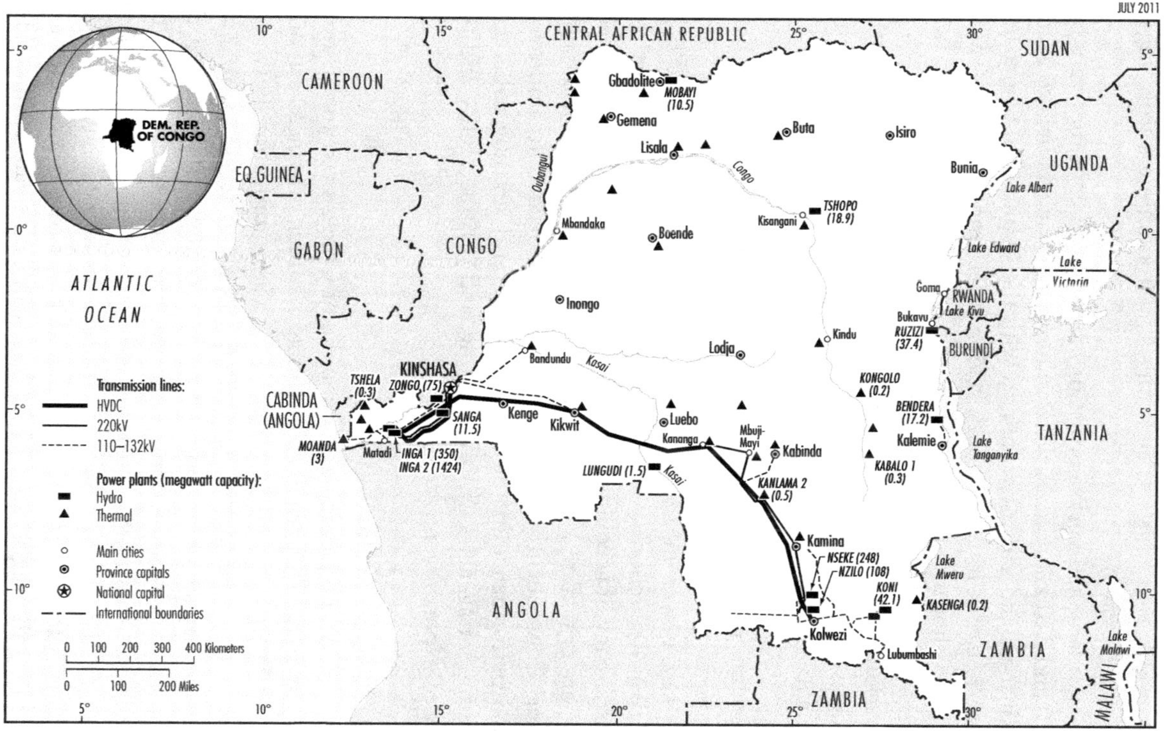

Source: Background paper, IV.1.

only about a quarter of its designed capacity. The system has three principal components that together span 5,547 kilometers:

- A 500 kilovolt HVDC line runs 1,740 kilometers from Inga to the Katanga region.
- Three large networks consist of high-voltage lines that vary between 50 and 220 kilovolts. A western network connects Inga to Matadi and Kinshasa and also interconnects with the Republic of Congo. A southern network in the Katanga region interconnects with Zambia. The HVDC line interconnects the southern and western networks. An eastern network interconnects with Burundi and Rwanda.
- Various independent mini-grids organized around smaller urban and industrial centers across the country are powered by small power plants.

Overall performance of the sector remains hampered by the lack of transparency in transactions. This, in turn, creates a climate of distrust. The key player in the sector is the Société Nationale d'Electricité (SNEL). Reduction in efficiency loss, transparency of export revenues, transparency of accounts, and staff downsizing in this state-owned enterprise are critical to achieving sustainable improvement in the electricity sector. Consequently, particular efforts are needed to improve operational performance in the following areas: (a) revenue collection from government agencies, (b) overstaffing, and (c) traceability and transparency of export revenues.

The Transport Sector
The bulk of the Democratic Republic of Congo's territory is not accessible by road. The provincial capitals of other provinces are only connected by road or air (see map 4.2). Communication between these capitals and other provincial centers (let alone access to rural areas) is often not possible. National unity and economic stability are the two top priorities for the country, and the transport sector is vital to both. The largest transport companies, either by employment, asset value, or turnover, are state-owned enterprises. Private operators of transport infrastructure and transport services do play a role in the sector, as exemplified by the registration of no less than 50 private airlines. However, most of these operators are small and undercapitalized; they escape any type of technical or economic regulation because of the informal nature of their operations.

Map 4.2   Transport Corridors

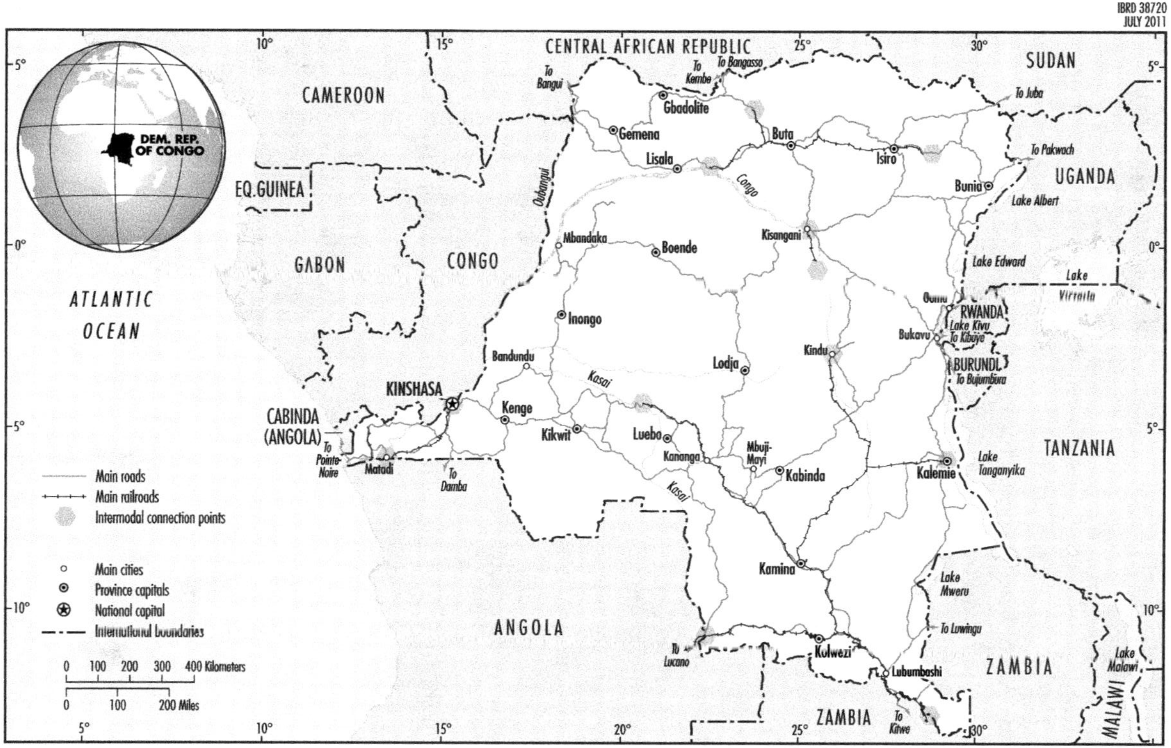

Source: Background paper, IV. 1.

In the Democratic Republic of Congo, transport activities managed by the state-owned enterprises generate about US$300 million or 2.8 percent of the country's GDP each year. The most prominent companies in the transport sector are the following (in alphabetical order):

- Chemin de Fer des Uélés is a rail network (currently not operational) in the northeastern part of the country, from Bumba to Mungbere, serving Aketi, Isiro, and Bondo.
- Direction des Voies de Desserte Agricoles is the parastatal agency that manages and maintains secondary and rural roads.
- Office des Routes manages and maintains the country's national and regional roads.
- Régie des Voies Aériennes (RVA) is the parastatal enterprise in charge of airport facilities and air traffic control.
- Régie des Voies Fluviales is the parastatal enterprise in charge of river waterways.
- Régie des Voies Maritimes is the parastatal enterprise in charge of seaways.
- Société Commerciale des Transports et des Ports (SCTP) is the commercial company for transportation and ports. It plays a key role in maritime transport, river transport, and rail transport.
- Société Nationale des Chemins de Fer du Congo (SNCC) is the national railways company.

For historic and geopolitical reasons, the transport sector was not built on market-oriented principles. It favored the establishment of state-owned enterprises with monopolies in subsector operations. Therefore, intramodal competition was not (and still is not) allowed in most subsectors where the state-owned enterprises are active, such as railways, seaport handling, and airport management. Competition from the informal sector, mainly road and river transportation, as well as from the formal aviation subsector, is strong and has an impact on state-owned transport enterprises. The diverse private airlines compete for the 1 million passengers and 280,000 tons of cargo a year generated by the domestic market.

As a consequence of weak accountability and poor governance, the transport sector's state-owned enterprises perform poorly compared to their peers in the region. Across the board, sector performance is suffering deeply from a lack of clarity on the assignment of revenue between the central and provincial levels. The issue goes further, however, as public procedures in the sector are subject to governance challenges. In the region, Uganda dealt with similar challenges by comparing its governance and accountability action plan to that of its peers (see box 4.1).

The Telecommunications Sector

In recent years the telecom sector has been one of the most dynamic economic sectors in the country. The telecom industry stimulates trade, creates jobs, generates wealth, and enhances social welfare. Mobile operators invested more than $500 million between 1998 and 2006 and contributed more than 6.7 percent of GDP in 2006 (compared with some 4 percent for the transportation sector and just over 10 percent for the mining industry). The telecom industry generated turnover of US$850 million in 2008: total revenue is shared roughly between Zain (US$380 million), Vodacom (US$330 million), and Tigo (US$80 million), and the rest is distributed between Congo China Telecom, Standard Telecom, and Supercel. Mobile operators in the Democratic Republic of Congo contributed fiscal revenues of more than US$160 million in 2008, compared to US$157 million and US$302 million, respectively, in Tanzania and Kenya.

Box 4.1

Lessons from Uganda's Experience with Governance in the Transport Sector

The Ugandan authorities compared the Transport Sector Development Project Governance and Accountability Action Plan of Uganda against the governance action plans of four projects outside of the Africa region (including three transport or road operations projects). The conclusion of the comparative analysis indicated that strengthening governance and accountability of investment projects in Africa may have to address the following: (a) corruption mapping in sectors, (b) disclosure provisions, (c) demand-side mitigation or civil society oversight of engagements with nongovernmental actors, (d) supply-side mitigation, (e) handling of complaints, (f) sanctions and remedies, and (g) implementation and monitoring of governance and accountability with regard to the action plan.

The fast-growing mobile phone market is replacing fixed-line telephony. The current operator, Office Congolais des Postes et Télécommunications (OCPT), was established in 1968 and is the sole provider of fixed lines. Its infrastructure is installed almost exclusively in the capital Kinshasa, with few lines available in other provincial cities. The land-line telephone network is almost completely depleted, with much of its equipment either out of date or broken. A private operator (Congo Korea Telecom) has started implementing a fiber-optic network in Kinshasa, connecting an estimated 3,000 subscribers. The cellular market has grown rapidly with the entrance of foreign investors. At the end of December 2001 an estimated 223,000 mobile subscribers were located across the country (equivalent to a 0.4 percent penetration rate); by the end of 2008, that number had jumped to around 9.4 million (a 15 percent penetration rate).

The Internet is available through private operators. OCPT is unable to offer Internet access, so several private companies have established niches by offering wireless services. There is no national fiber-optic backbone in the country, and the absence of a broadband connection is the main infrastructural obstacle to the proliferation of information and communication technologies. All Internet service providers in the country use satellites, except for Congo Korea Telecom, which uses fiber optics to connect its offices to its clients in Kinshasa. The principal Internet service providers operate in the big cities (Kinshasa, Mbuji-Mayi, and Lubumbashi, in particular) and on the mining sites. Internet service providers work mostly with business customers, as the residential market is estimated at less than 10,000 subscribers. Internet tariffs are some US$100 a month for a connection of 64 kilobytes per second because of the cost of access to international bandwidth (exclusively by satellite).

Plans are in place for implementing a sector and broadband strategy. In May 2009 it was announced that Renatelsat, part of the OCPT, would form a public-private partnership with China International Telecommunication Construction, part of China Communications Services Corporation, to lay down a US$274 million satellite and ter-restrial wireless-based network across the country. The government also launched the construction of a fiber-optic backbone linking Kinshasa to Muanda on the Atlantic coast. The electricity provider SNEL also plans to complement its electricity transmission cable to Zambia with a tele-com backbone. The latter could also offer access to undersea cables and global information communications technology networks. The expansion of this large project will create not only economic opportunities but also major governance challenges, balancing national interests with private corporate interests.

Impact of the Lack of Infrastructure

Large companies in the Democratic Republic of Congo are increasingly establishing and managing their own infrastructure, circumventing the absence of public services. Almost all companies employing 100 or more people have their own generators, and only 39 percent of these companies consider the lack of electricity to be a serious obstacle to growth. By contrast, only a third of companies employing fewer than 20 people own generators, and the majority of those companies consider the lack of electricity to be a serious obstacle. At the household level, generators are rare, and the lack of electricity is a serious concern for almost everybody. As for transport, a small share of the population has access to air travel, while long-distance overland transport hardly exists. Most of the population must rely on public services, and these involve state-owned companies.

The lack of infrastructure reinforces national, provincial, and within-cities isolation. As highlighted in chapter 2, isolation is the principal outgrowth of the country's poor economic performance. A key contributor to this geographic and economic isolation is the lack of infrastructure. Within cities, already affected by looting and war, lack of investment in infrastructure, combined with lack of maintenance, has led to deterioration of the transportation network and limited the population's access to electricity and water, with serious impacts on the country's human development indicators. Unreliable transportation thwarts access to employment (see chapter 5 of this report) and the development of the private sector.

Investment Priorities

Infrastructure investments by the Democratic Republic of Congo attest to the government's state-building priorities. The state's objectives are to construct and operate infrastructure that (a) connects the regions and provinces, (b) provides access to international markets, and (c) demonstrates the capacity of the state to deliver services. To realize these objectives, the state has incurred large costs, both in financial outlays and in the opportunity cost of alternative developments.

Identifying the priorities for infrastructure investments continues to be a challenge. Competing interests and political agendas are influencing the identification of priority investments. In a context of limited investments, clarifying those priorities that have the strongest potential has yielded the following list:

- *Connectivity of provinces.* The development of corridors that connect the provinces has been prioritized over the development of urban areas. There has been a continual debate among Congolese authorities and external partners about which corridors should be prioritized. Economic analysis suggests that some corridors, notably the corridor from Kinshasa to the Atlantic Ocean (through Matadi and Pointe Noire) and the Congo River corridor from Kinshasa to Kisangani, can indeed be developed with high economic returns if the construction of roads, telecommunications, and power connectivity is bundled together at the same time. The economic rates of return to an integrated connection from Kinshasa to Lubumbashi are much lower, but recognize the historical and political importance of this connection (see for example, Young and Turner 1985). Some development partners may shift the priorities by funding a specific component of the selected corridors, raising the economic rates of return on other components of these corridors. For example, development of the Inga III hydroelectric dam and related aluminum smelter would significantly raise the rate of return on a deepwater port at Banana.

- *Access to international markets.* The airports in Goma and Bukavu and a deepwater port at Banana are favored for development, while the government could also opt to use the facilities in neighboring countries (Rwanda and the Republic of Congo, respectively), provided the risks are managed properly. Institutional arrangements may provide some insurance. The development of the East African Community ensures inland countries of their continued access to deepwater ports in neighboring countries. Insurance from commercial companies and the Multilateral Investment Guarantee Agency could reduce the financial risk of politically motivated interference by neighboring governments.

- *Competition of various alternative supply routes.* The congested port of Matadi is the only major conduit supplying Kinshasa. Private operators are evaluating two alternative routes: (a) supplying Kinshasa through the Mombasa–Kisangani–Congo River connection, once the river markings allow round-the-clock transport and regulatory issues have been addressed, and (b) the Pointe Noire–Brazzaville road and rail connection, once it is fully operational.

- *Demonstration of the capacity of the state.* Bundling infrastructure projects and ensuring the safety and security of property in selected "growth poles" are proposed for the special economic zone at N'Sele near Kinshasa. This collective effort is designed to demonstrate the capacity of the state to deliver, through a private sector operator, good governance by means of the effective management of infrastructure. The challenge of this initiative is to ensure that good governance and service delivery are continued over time. Here it may help to anchor the growth pole in a regional agreement to ensure the continued commitment of the Congolese government and its neighbors.

An alternative arrangement has been used to prioritize fiscal resources for infrastructure investments in the Democratic Republic of Congo. Investments have been growing rapidly since 2008, starting from a very low starting point (one of the lowest levels of per capita public investment expenditures in Africa; see figure 4.1). Most of this expansion has been funded by an agreement between the Democratic Republic of Congo and China under a type of resources-for-infrastructure swap. The agreement established a joint venture between the state-owned mining company Gécamines and two Chinese companies to exploit a mining site in Katanga; the revenue from this concession would first repay the investment in the mine itself and thereafter repay loans that the Chinese Export Import Bank provides to fund infrastructure projects selected by the Congolese authorities. The main features of this agreement are as follows:

- Repayment of the loans is guaranteed by specific mining revenues, and this has raised the Democratic Republic of Congo's creditworthiness. A government guarantee can only be called after 25 years; the grant element of the loan is 47 percent.
- Financial resources are managed outside normal budgetary procedures and could be safeguarded for capital spending. In contrast, regular revenues are typically used for current spending, notably public sector wages.
- Capital spending could be prioritized for state-building efforts and excluded from regular cost-benefit analysis. All things being equal, this raises the macroeconomic risk of debt distress.

The selected projects are not subject to regular public procurement procedures, which could undermine the cost-effectiveness of their implementation. Chinese partners have no economic interest in effective

Figure 4.1   Public Investment in the Democratic Republic of Congo and Select Countries

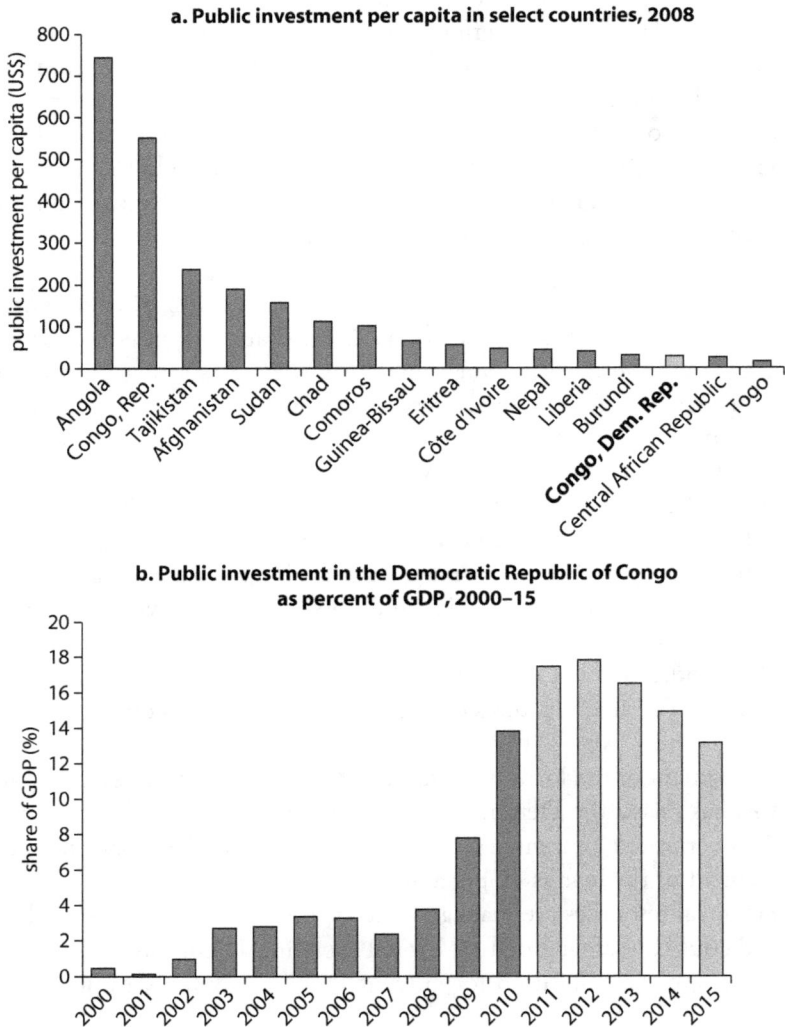

a. Public investment per capita in select countries, 2008

b. Public investment in the Democratic Republic of Congo as percent of GDP, 2000–15

Source: a. Background paper. II.2; b. Authors' calculation from central bank and International Monetary Fund data.

implementation because mining revenues guarantee repayment of the loans. Selection of projects on noneconomic criteria may complicate the mobilization of resources to maintain the newly constructed infrastructure. And even projects selected on economic criteria need to account for future maintenance to ensure continued benefits.

State-Owned Enterprises and Service Delivery

The authorities are well aware of the need to reform state-owned companies to improve public services. Since 2007, the authorities have made significant progress in clarifying the legal framework that applies to state-owned enterprises. In July 2008 the legal framework for state disengagement from public enterprises was revamped, transforming state-owned enterprises into commercial companies (subject to common law), public establishments, or public services; enterprises that were not operational or were insolvent were to be liquidated. By end-2010 all state-owned enterprises had been transferred into the appropriate legal structure to conform to the law; 20 of the most important had been selected to become commercial companies. The next steps of this program require dealing with the social liabilities of these enterprises, which are estimated to amount to some US$670 million in the six main state-owned enterprises: Gécamines (mining), Regideso (water and sanitation), SNEL (electricity), SCTP (water and rail transport), SNCC (railways), and RVA (airports and air control). However, there is no labor adjustment program in the public enterprise reform effort, and a strategy either would be costly or might require amendments to the Congolese Labor Law of 2002.

The reform of the legal framework is only the first step. In practice, implementation of the reform of state-owned enterprises remains difficult and requires careful prioritization. The authorities appear to have adopted a pragmatic approach regarding the following sector-specific principles:

- Natural monopolies are being reformed as ongoing companies. For example, the state railway company is valuable if operated as a single company, and it would be difficult to manage its subsidiaries as separate companies.[3] By contrast, the economies of scale of maintaining the state water company, Regideso, are not obvious. The separate companies that make up Regideso may be managed more efficiently as stand-alone activities. This was confirmed by the lack of interest from private companies in managing Regideso as a single national company. By contrast, potential operators appear interested in managing smaller companies that constitute the national company.

- All state-owned enterprises can improve their efficiency by subcontracting specific activities to the private sector. Such subcontracting can take various forms. In the telecom sector, private mobile companies deliver practically all services once they obtain an exemption from the legal requirement that only OCPT can deliver certain services.

The success of these companies appears to be specific to some of the technical features, which may be difficult to replicate in other infrastructure sectors, but feasible in some mobile banking services (see box 4.2). In river transport, SCTP delivers the bulk of cross-border transport between Kinshasa and Brazzaville, consistent with its monopoly. In practice, this allows a private company to deliver high-quality services for paying customers.

Models for adequate funding, management, and maintenance of basic infrastructure and services will have to be tailored to specific sectors. The reform of the legal status of state-owned enterprises as well as the identification of sources of investment will be implemented along different tracks.

- *Public management funded by user charges is based on sound economics but is institutionally challenging.* An example is the national road fund; resources that should have been used for maintenance were diverted to investment and administration.
- *Publicly funded but privately managed systems function well in some sectors but have removed the incentives for efficiency gains in privately managed activities.* Airport maintenance fees are mobilized by the Ministry of Finance but managed by RVA. This model has allowed an expansion

Box 4.2

The Telecom Sector: Key Elements That Supported Its Rapid Growth

- *Prepayment.* All mobile telephone services are prepaid, and hence there is no creditor risk.
- *Continual service benefits.* Even during the war in the Great Lakes region, telecom towers survived largely unscathed, as all parties relied on mobile phones. Armed groups that might have destroyed a mobile telephone tower would have disconnected their own telephone. Implicitly, there was a consensus that such installations would not be damaged because all stakeholders received *continual* benefits.
- *Inability to misappropriate service during transmission.* By contrast, power and water services require overland transmission that can be diverted, and hence predation is more difficult to prevent.

of airport services, but the same expansion might have been financed by efficiency gains if the operation had been fully privately owned.

- *Privately mobilized and managed systems subject to public oversight are desirable in principle but challenging in the Democratic Republic of Congo, as the regulator tends to be "captured" by the private party.* This model has long been applied to the management of religious schools and is now being considered for the delivery of infrastructure services. The experience with the education system demonstrates the difficulties in regulating a powerful nongovernmental partner (see box 4.3).
- *Full privatization without public oversight is feasible if there is competition between private operators.* The successful expansion of the telecom sector is based on this model. The same approach may be applied to alternative corridors linking Kinshasa to the coast.

Box 4.3

Public-Private Partnership in the Education Sector

The Congolese education system is characterized by a strong disequilibrium between secular (23.5 percent) and religiously affiliated (76.5 percent) public schools (Ministry of Education of the Democratic Republic of Congo 2009); the proportion of private schools in the system is estimated at 11 percent. This polarity dates from colonial times. On the eve of national independence (1960), official (*écoles officielles*) and independent (*écoles libres*) schools existed side by side (in reality, the situation was even more complicated with regard to finance and administration, including official, conventional official, and independent schools). The first were established and financed by the government; the second were established and operated by nongovernmental bodies, mainly Roman Catholic and Protestant missions. After independence, long-standing and tense church-state relationships resulted in the nationalization (*étatisation*) of all religious schools in 1974. Three years later, both parties reached consensus on a redefined regulatory framework, called *La Convention*: the state would remain in the driver's seat (*pouvoir organisateur*) but agreed to give churches large oversight power (*gestion*) of their respective schools. In other words, the religious networks would remain part of the public system, and their schools would be financed and controlled by the government. In practice, however, roles and responsibilities were unclear. As a result, religious networks continue operating more or less as autonomous, parallel

(continued next page)

Box 4.3 *(continued)*

structures inside the public system. This de facto fine line between "public" and "private" generates opportunities but also poses challenges.

The hybrid nature of the system gave religious networks room to cope with the dramatic decline in public expenditures on education in the mid-1980s. The Catholic network, in particular, was the driving force behind the controversial *prime de motivation* (teacher salary top-up paid by households) policy that eventually put an end to teacher strikes in the early 1990s. In doing so, the Church bypassed the state, arguing that it had failed to fulfill its obligations. The current system of school fees (with its elaborate quotas allocated to different administrative structures) is a product of this murky institutional arrangement. The *coup de force* initiated by the Church presumably not only prevented the education system from total collapse but also ensured the survival of the religious institutions themselves, increasingly confronted with a lack of financial support from their base congregations abroad. Ironically, the major beneficiary of fees raised to finance the operating costs of administrative offices is the secular network (72 percent); religious networks, which run three-quarters of all public schools, only take in 28 percent. What had started as a unilateral move has long since been institutionalized. As of 2009, households financed at least 37 percent of the education budget, the state financed 48 percent, and other sources financed 15 percent. (Government of the Democratic Republic of Congo 2010b).

The proliferation of administrative structures and networks (for example, Protestants have 19 different communities in Bandundu Province alone) is a direct result of the negotiation power of churches at the time of *La Convention* (1977), when they managed to preserve their own "private" structures inside the public system (offices at national, provincial, and local levels; parallel inspection teams). Initially limited to four major religious groups (Catholic, Protestant, Kimbanguist, and Islamic), there are now up to 15 registered national offices (*coordinations nationales*). Hence, this expansion not only raises issues of duplication or the development of parallel structures, it also represents a substantial cost for the state (salaries, operating costs) and the parents (school fees). Further, their influential position enables religious networks to take unilateral decisions. For instance, in 2009, the Catholic Church created a Solidarity Fund (*Fonds de Solidarité*) to better regulate the collection of school fees in the town of Kinshasa. At that time, government and donors were strongly committed to preparing a strategy for reducing school fees via an extensive consultation process, but they were not associated with the initiative of the Catholic Church. Fees tripled in many Catholic primary schools in Kinshasa.

Notes

1. In addition, Inga III is a proposed 4,320 megawatt run-of-river hydropower facility to be located at the Inga Falls on the Congo River. Commercial operation is projected in about 10 years, and, as currently contemplated, power output will be used for both domestic demand and export to the South African Power Pool. The site currently hosts the smaller Inga I and II generators. On October 26, 2010, the Ministry of Energy published a call for expressions of interest for the detailed engineering, development, construction, and operation of the Inga III power plant with a view to prequalifying experienced developers and investors; the project will be developed as a public-private partnership with majority private shareholding and BHP Billiton as an anchor customer (for its proposed aluminum smelter requiring between 1,500 and 2,000 megawatts) and also possibly as a minority shareholder. However, prior studies are required on hydrology, geology, environment, structuring and risk assessment of the public-private partnership, and legal aspects, before the government can reach an agreement with a developer and BHP Billiton. Since Inga III as currently designed hinges on the aluminum smelter being built in the Bas Congo Province, the risks associated with this project as well as adequate pricing of electricity (at no lower than Inga III's average cost, currently estimated at US$0.35 per kilowatt-hour) should also be assessed. The authorities are considering inviting the World Bank and other development partners to support this process.

2. Total annual electricity production in 2009 was around 7,500 gigawatt-hours, or less than 50 percent of what the installed capacity could potentially generate. Currently, available capacity at Inga I and II totals about 8,000 megawatts. With demand exceeding capacity during peak hours, there is regular shedding of load in Kinshasa, and the gap between demand and generation capacity is widening. Some of the smaller hydropower facilities are wholly inoperative, and only about a third of the small thermal power plants function. As a result, electricity supply from the grid has been completely cut off in urban centers in remote regions.

3. Since June 2010, restructuring of the state railway company, SNCC, has been supported by the World Bank Multi-Modal Transport Project.

CHAPTER 5

Private Sector Development and Employment Creation

The Democratic Republic of Congo has a young, rapidly growing population that is eager for employment opportunities. The formal private sector, excluding recently converted state-owned enterprises, may generate as few as 300,000 jobs, 1.2 percent of the workforce. The remainder is forced to engage in subsistence farming or in the informal sector. The situation has not improved substantially since 2006. Income levels in agriculture are rising but do not generate demand for skilled labor. Developments in the informal sector have fluctuated over time, and the crisis of 2008–09 hit the urban poor particularly hard because of exchange rate movements that were not compensated by income opportunities.

The Congolese government is aware of the structural constraints to private sector development. The lack of coordination of government agencies has slowed progress in trade facilitation, tax collection, and legal reform and has stalled the development of a competitive telecommunications banking sector. This chapter reviews the progress of some important reforms and discusses the ways that innovative institutional arrangements, such as public-private partnerships and external anchors, as well as new technologies can help to remove the impediments to reform.

Employment

The country's turbulent history has forced its population to deal with a wide range of challenges. During and immediately after the war, formal employment offered little economic support, as wages were paid irregularly, if at all. Both formal and informal employees developed coping strategies to deal with the employment, income, and security challenges. As the situation normalized, those with formal employment could rely on labor market protection policies; therefore, formal employment is discussed first, although it covers only a very small fraction of total employment.

The Formal Sector: A Limited Source of Employment

The formal sector of the Congolese economy is rather small. Apart from the state-owned enterprises, it contains mostly small to medium-size Congolese enterprises and a small number of large foreign-owned enterprises. Many of these larger enterprises are active in the mining and telecom sectors.

State-owned enterprises dominate a significant part of the Congolese economy. To support their reform, the government set up the Comité de Pilotage de la Reforme des Entreprises du Portefeuille de l'État (COPIREP) as the main executive agency. In 2007 COPIREP was responsible for 53 public enterprises and 65 enterprises in mixed ownership. The enterprises in both categories are active in a variety of sectors, and their respective financial states range from bankruptcy to moderate success. Projects have been launched to reform three companies in the transport sector, two in the infrastructure sector, one in the mining sector, one in industry, and one in telecommunications. Another six enterprises were identified for priority action, but no diagnostic assessment is available at this time. State-owned enterprises have a monopoly in certain business sectors, particularly water and electricity supply and railroad transportation. The major state-owned enterprises employ between 5,000 and 12,000 people each; other state-owned enterprises are considerably smaller.

The Informal Sector

It is hard to determine what constitutes informality in the context of the Democratic Republic of Congo (see box 5.1). Most studies label companies as "informal" based either on firm size (for example, fewer than five

Box 5.1

The 2010 Investment Climate Assessment Survey

In 2010 an Investment Climate Assessment (ICA) Survey was conducted in the Democratic Republic of Congo. As part of the survey 304 companies were interviewed using a standard World Bank survey that allows international comparison of results. The survey covered small companies employing fewer than 20 staff, medium-size companies employing 20–100 staff, and larger companies employing more than 100 staff (see table B5.1). The results of the survey update a similar, but more narrow, survey that was conducted in 2006. The results of the 2010 survey are discussed in Background paper, IV.3.

Table B5.1   Results of the 2010 Investment Climate Assessment Survey

Sector and location, by size of firm	Mean number of workers	Mean age of firm	Mean years in formal sector	Number of observations
Sector				
Manufacturing				
Small	6.4	10.3	4.4	162
Medium	50.4	18.4	17.8	25
Large	286.9	41.0	39.0	13
Service				
Small	7.8	12.4	9.0	142
Medium	46.5	80.4	17.2	19
Large	577.2	29.6	27.8	14
Location				
Out of Kinshasa				
Small	7.1	11.2	6.5	172
Medium	41.7	127.5	13.4	6
Large	183.0	87.0	87.0	0
Kinshasa				
Small	7.3	11.9	7.4	132
Medium	51.0	20.2	19.0	38
Large	455.8	33.2	31.0	27

Source: 2010 ICA Survey.
Note: Small firms employ fewer than 20 employees, medium-size firms employ between 20 and 100 employees, and large firms employ more than 100 employees.

employees) or on registration status (see table 5.1). In the Democratic Republic of Congo, it is unclear whether small enterprises holding a "patent" should be considered formal or informal. Inherent in any study of informal sector activity is that data are difficult to obtain and often

Table 5.1   Perceived Obstacles to Registration, 2006 and 2010

Obstacles to registration	Percent of enterprises that considered this a major obstacle, 2006	Percent of enterprises that ranked this as the most severe obstacle, 2010
No benefit to formality	—	32.0
Taxes on registered businesses	57.8	26.7
Lacking information on procedures	12.0	14.0
Fees to complete registration	43.3	10.7
Time to complete registration	12.4	8.7
Potential inspections and bureaucracy	51.9	0.7

Source: 2010 ICA Survey.
— Not available.

unreliable, although some estimates provide an approximation of the sector's size and importance.

The informal sector is barely monitored, but available data highlight its prevalence. A study conducted in 2004 by the Institut National de Statistique in the Kinshasa region counted almost 540,000 nonregistered enterprises in the capital alone, producing an annual value added of CGF 485 billion. These informal enterprises generated 692,000 jobs, which accounted for 70 percent of employment in the region, compared with 12 percent for the formal private sector and 17 percent for the public sector. These numbers are in line with estimates for other countries in Sub-Saharan Africa. The conclusion is that the informal sector accounts for between 60 and 80 percent of business activity in many countries. The 2006 Investment Climate Assessment (ICA) Survey suggests an even higher share of informal activity—in the range of 90 percent of all business activity—and found that the majority of informal enterprises were engaged in retail and commercial activities (63.2 percent), followed by industrial and manufacturing activities (14.8 percent) and services (12.3 percent). The 2004 study found that most enterprises involved a single entrepreneur and usually no employees, which points to subsistence activities.

Rate of Sector-Specific Employment, Status, and Opportunities

The construction sector could become an important employer in the Democratic Republic of Congo. According to the 1-2-3 Household Survey, the construction sector, including housing construction, employed 71,000 people in 2005.[1] Data on employment in large-scale construction (roads, large infrastructure) are sparse. Given the ambitious list of infra-structure projects under implementation or awaiting implementation, the construction sector is likely to grow over the next several years.

The deterioration of the education system has made it difficult for companies in the construction sector to recruit qualified staff. Skilled and semiskilled workers (especially mechanics, metal workers, and technicians), managers, and intermediaries (foremen, yard bosses) have been difficult to find. The shortage of skills is particularly acute in the case of middle managers, because training is lacking. Despite the general degradation of the education system over the past 20 years, the Democratic Republic of Congo has been able to maintain an adequate supply of engineers with basic engineering skills; however, there are shortages of engineers with knowledge of new technologies. The same issue also applies to skilled mechanics.

The agriculture sector is an important source of employment.[2] More than 10 million people were involved in the agriculture sector in 2005, and it is possible that this number reached 15 million in 2010. The potential for expansion in this sector is substantial, especially if thousands of abandoned farms are refurbished. The country has about 80 million square hectares of arable nonforest land, only 10 percent of which is currently under production. If this land were properly cultivated, the country could become a significant net exporter of food (FAO, UNFPA, and IIASA 1984). At the moment, however, the agriculture sector is languishing, and the country is a net importer of food. There are also important opportunities for cash crops; in the past, the country has been an important producer of palm oil, rubber, sugar, coffee, and cotton (Background paper, III.1). Increased production in these sectors would lead to a dramatic expansion in employment, a reduction in poverty, a more diversified base of exports, and a more reliable foreign exchange position. This would require investing in capital and mechanization, which would boost productivity, as well as in the planting and harvesting of crops on new land. Finally, investment in new seeds could boost agricultural productivity and double or even triple yields.

Although geographically limited, the mining sector is an important source of employment in certain regions. Dominated by a few large firms (Gécamines, Societé Minière de Bakwanga, and joint-venture partners), it is mostly active in Katanga, the two Kasai provinces, and some eastern provinces. The exact level of employment is unknown. World Bank estimates vary between 500,000 and 2 million formal and informal workers (see World Bank 2010a). Further, fluctuations in the mining sector have important spillover effects in the mining regions, which may lead to fluctuations in employment in other sectors, as local demand rises and falls. Because of inadequate training, the shortage of skilled workers is a drag on productivity: approximately 10 workers are required to do the same work that could be done by one engineer in Western Europe.[3]

Cross-Cutting Constraints to Formal Employment

A weak businesses climate has prevented the private sector from creating jobs. The obstacles to job creation include insufficient public services and infrastructure, limited human capital and access to financing, regulatory hurdles, state enterprise monopolies, and uncertain land rights. The Democratic Republic of Congo is ranked 175 out of 183 in the 2011 Doing Business ranking. The challenges are similar but more severe in the Democratic Republic of Congo than in other developing countries. For example, in 2006 Congolese enterprises reported an average of 19 power outages a month, resulting in losses of 7 percent of annual sales—much higher than in comparable neighboring countries. This affected small and medium-size companies disproportionately because they generally lacked in-house generators. In 2010 the figures were even worse, with an average of 23 power outages a month and losses of 19 percent of annual sales.

The Democratic Republic of Congo is notorious for the low penetration of its banking sector, with approximately 200,000 bank accounts for a population of some 67 million people. The regression analysis indicates a solid correlation between productivity-sales and access to banking services (using several different variables), although data do not identify causality (Background paper, IV.3). The 2010 ICA Survey also found that small and medium-size enterprises consider access to credit to be the most important constraint to growth. This is an indirect effect of poor protection of property rights. Banks do not lend in an environment where creditor rights are not enforced, and in the Democratic Republic of Congo, nonperforming loans reached 20 percent in 2009. Enforcement of good laws and regulations is an uphill challenge because of ineffective state governance (see chapter 3).

Private sector development has been hobbled by myriad taxes and levies, both formal and informal. Formal tax requirements are inefficient, but informal tax requirements, which are generated at all levels of government and by an array of agencies and officials, are a bigger problem for private sector enterprises. Myriad taxes and levies are extorted from private sector enterprises. Large enterprises, for the most part, have succeeded in insulating themselves from corruption and continue to prosper. Smaller and medium-size corporations, however, do not have the means or political clout to thwart such extortion. These companies remain tightly subdued by a heavy framework of ambiguous regulations that give rise to extensive harassment. Consequently, employment by small and medium-size companies has grown little in recent years.[4]

Exports, Employment, and Trade Facilitation

Exports offer economic opportunities to the rapidly growing labor force. Demand is rising for agricultural commodities, as demonstrated by rising food prices on international markets. Delays at the border are the biggest impediment to exports of perishable goods. Exports of agricultural products offer employment opportunities for the unskilled to the highly skilled, allowing for continuous growth as skills become more sophisticated and incomes rise over time. In the Democratic Republic of Congo some established firms are experienced exporters and are ready to expand production and exports when trade facilitation improves (Background paper, V.2). Further, these firms can leverage their experience by subcontracting to formal and informal companies. Similarly, agricultural concessions, once revived, could contribute to employment directly and through subcontracting to suppliers.

The Democratic Republic of Congo's trade facilitation practices limit formal sector employment growth. Trade facilitation procedures are complicated and time-consuming because all agencies prefer to collect their own fees directly from traders. Trade is slower, more expensive, and much riskier for traders in the Democratic Republic of Congo than in other countries in Africa and beyond. Cross-border procedures take, on average, 44 days for exports and 63 days for imports, which are 12 and 15 days longer, respectively, than the average for Sub-Saharan Africa. Average costs are close to US$3,500 per container for both imports and exports, well above the average for Sub-Saharan Africa (see figure 5.1; Background paper, V.1). The risks are also much higher than elsewhere: port time in Matadi is unpredictable, and small traders in the Great Lakes region report various forms of harassment and human rights abuses. The risks, delays, and high costs discourage otherwise competitive exports.

Poor trade facilitation procedures also stunt the growth of income in urban areas, particularly in Kinshasa and the eastern border towns of Goma and Bukavu. Economic growth in these urban areas is important not only for poverty alleviation but also for social and political stability. Regional integration would offer economies of scale and more efficient use of space and services (see chapter 4).[5] The economic benefits of regional integration go beyond the financial benefits of reducing the cost of infrastructure. For example, Kinshasa and Brazzaville are geographically a single economic entity, but they are currently separated by the regulatory costs

Figure 5.1   Indicators of Uncertainty in Cross-Border Transactions in Select Regions

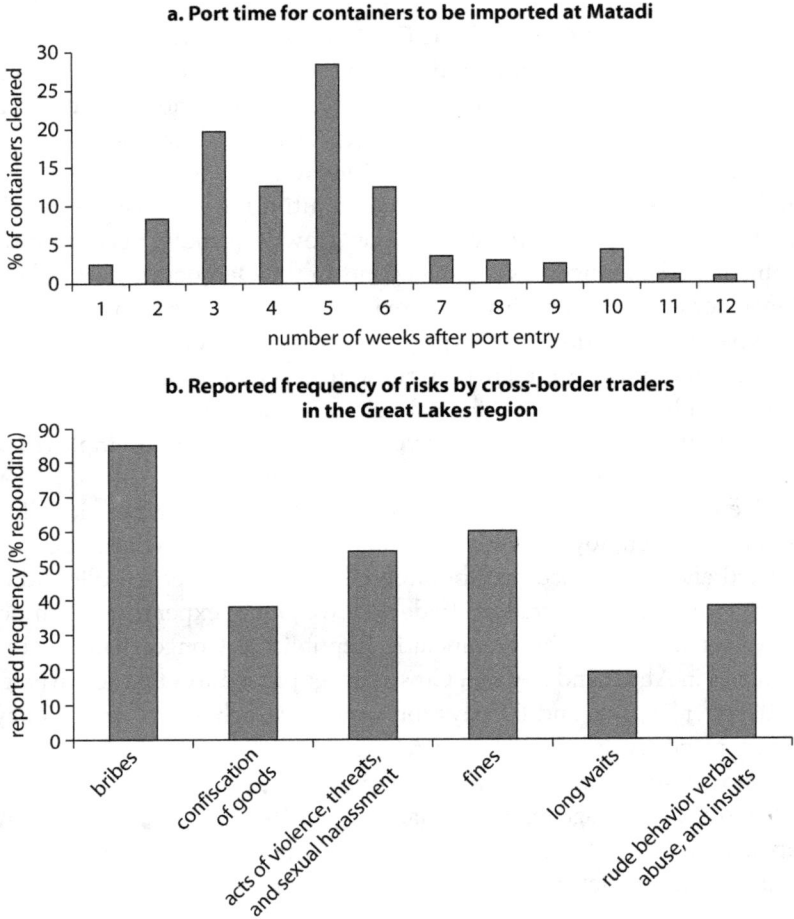

a. Port time for containers to be imported at Matadi

b. Reported frequency of risks by cross-border traders in the Great Lakes region

Source: Background paper, V.1.

of intracity trade. Surveys in both cities show that private sector firms are eager for improved trade facilitation procedures and lower transport costs (see table 5.2).

Service Delivery through Public Partnerships, Starting with Trade Facilitation

The key to improving trade facilitation procedures is to find an institutional arrangement that is trusted by all parties. If all border payments were delegated to a central "single window" and inspections were carried

Table 5.2   Estimated Impact of Improved Border Procedures at the Kinshasa-Brazzaville Border

% increase in trade volume for a 50% fall in costs or delays

Trade indicator	Transport costs	Administrative costs	Border delays
All exports			
Mean	102	79	12.5
Median	37.5	25	5
N	12	12	10
All imports			
Mean	31	39	17
Median	20	25	10
N	36	39	29

Source: Background paper, V.3.

out on a risk assessment basis, border procedures could be significantly accelerated (Government of the Democratic Republic of Congo 2010a). An external anchor could enhance the credibility of single-window trade facilitation operators and the creation of special economic zones. The planned single-window contractor is expected to be a joint venture with a foreign company that would adhere to international accounting practices. Indications are that such an arrangement has improved coordination in other countries (see box 5.2).

Legal Protection for Economic Activities and Employment

This section discusses the economic costs of legal uncertainty, the reform path selected by the authorities, and the challenges in implementing it.

Economic Costs of Legal Uncertainty

The legal uncertainties of doing business in the Democratic Republic of Congo are elevated. On the Doing Business index of contract enforcement, the country is ranked 172 out of 183 countries. On average, it takes 43 procedures and 625 days to enforce a contract, and the cost typically exceeds the value of the claim by more than 50 percent. The high costs of contract enforcement in Congolese courts results in large contracts typically going to arbitration by foreign panels. Such panels are expensive and time-consuming and consequently rare. Companies with smaller contract issues do not have this option and are essentially excluded from legal recourse to enforcement. This is expected to change once the legislation needed to comply with the Organization for the Harmonization of Business Law in Africa (OHADA) Treaty is in place

Box 5.2

Alternatives to Relieving Binding Constraints to Trade, Investment, and Growth

Trade and investment typically depend on a requisite set of public services, notably at the regulatory level. Failure to provide these services imposes binding constraints on growth. Many fragile or postconflict states have trouble providing these services. Even for governments that recognize binding constraints to growth, reforming public sector functionality may not be feasible politically, capacity may be lacking, or the timing may not be right. Consequently, governments concerned with boosting growth have resorted to innovative public-private partnerships, such as contracting out, in an effort to relieve some of these constraints. Various governments have taken notable measures to relieve the constraints to trade and investment:

- *Outsourcing of customs in Indonesia.* Following the commodity price shocks of the early 1980s, Indonesia's leadership recognized the need to strengthen labor-intensive industries such as textile exports (see Temple 2001). However, customs were clearly seen as a binding constraint, subjecting both importers and exporters to significant delays and transaction costs. Since export industries such as textiles were also highly dependent on imported inputs, this throttled the development of the industry. In 1986 the government effectively outsourced the inspection of imports by Indonesian customs with Swiss General Surveyor. The arrangements were maintained for more than two decades, contributing to the significant expansion of Indonesia's export-oriented manufacturing sector.

- *Special processing zones.* The Chinese government has focused on developing special economic zones (Wei 1999), which typically provide export-oriented firms with a package of reliable infrastructure services such as electricity, water, and sanitation as well as special regulatory procedures. These are typically more business friendly and targeted at particular industries than the rest of the country. The Democratic Republic of Congo plans to build its first special economic zone in the Kinshasa district of N'Sélé. It would be operative in 2012 and dedicated to agro-industries.

- *Concessions for infrastructural services.* In Cambodia, the postconflict government used licensing and concession arrangements to provide a wide array of public services and infrastructure. Concessions were given to private enterprises for garbage collection in Angkor Wat and Phnom Penh; road building and maintenance in provinces; and development of airports, Internet service providers, and voice-over-Internet protocol (Rondinelli 2006, 9).

(continued next page)

Box 5.2 *(continued)*

- *Nongovernmental support for sectoral growth.* Much emphasis has been placed on the role of donors and nongovernmental organizations (NGOs) in supporting key social sectors. In Rwanda the Ministry of Agriculture has worked with a series of NGOs to provide key inputs and extension services to farmers (Rondinelli 2006).

  In these examples, governments have sought to address binding constraints to trade, investment, and growth by using mechanisms outside the traditional functioning of government. While innovative, such approaches also entail challenges. The first concerns sustainability. Longer-term strategies need to ensure that these functions will be mainstreamed back into the core public sector or will be sustained in other forms. Most important, these types of arrangements require credible conditions in which the public sector works with nongovernmental agents. As with all public-private partnerships, they require specific capacities in government. While the benefits of these types of arrangements can be significant, they are no silver bullet.

because its dispute settlement provisions are cheaper than commercial international arbitration procedures.

The absence of legal recourse to enforce contracts has had adverse effects on employment creation and fiscal revenues:

- Lack of legal resources to ensure repayment reduces the availability of credit. Even some 20 percent of the carefully selected debtors default on their loans (IMF 2010). The credit constraint applies disproportionately to small companies; large companies generally have access to credit from foreign suppliers or owners. The 2010 ICA Survey lists the absence of credit as the most important obstacle to growth, affecting 40 percent of companies, up from 14 percent in 2006. The reluctance of banks to lend can be explained by the high cost to enforce contracts.[6]

- Even large firms find it difficult and costly to challenge state authorities in court. For small companies the costs are prohibitive. Small companies typically resort to making unofficial payments to avoid a challenge by the tax or other official authorities. The cost of these payments has hampered the emergence and growth of competitive small and medium-size companies, which typically generate more than half of total employment.

- Legal uncertainty has also discouraged foreign direct investment and trade. Investment and trade play an important role in providing access to up-to-date technology, which is necessary for growth and for fiscal revenues.

The authorities' strategy is simultaneously to update the laws and strengthen enforcement. External anchors, such as the OHADA Treaty, the New York Arbitration Convention of 1958, and regional institutions such as the South African Development Community and the East African Community could play an important role in this strategy.[7] To succeed, these treaties require complementary national legislation. Further, the Congolese authorities need to face squarely their constitutional obligations, and effective implementation remains under national control. They consider the establishment of commercial courts and the training of judges and other officials to be a priority. We discuss them in that order.

Leverage to Reduce Legal Uncertainty

The OHADA uniform laws will become law in the Democratic Republic of Congo 60 days after the treaty is signed (establishing supremacy over existing laws). By harmonizing business law, the treaty seeks to promote regional integration and economic growth and to ensure a secure legal environment. The treaty has the following uniform laws:

- General commercial law
- Corporate law and rules concerning different types of joint ventures
- Laws concerning secured transactions (guarantees and collateral)
- Debt recovery and enforcement law
- Bankruptcy law
- Arbitration law
- Accounting law
- Law regulating contracts for the carriage of goods by road

These laws can be amended upon agreement of the OHADA legislative body, which consists of the Council of Ministers of Justice and Finance of the member states.[8] A Common Court of Justice and Arbitration allows both member states and private parties to come before the court after national procedures have been exhausted. The court (1) advises on the uniform application and interpretation of the common OHADA business law, (2) reviews decisions rendered by courts of appeal of the member states in cases involving the application of OHADA business law, and

(3) monitors the arbitration proceedings conducted pursuant to the OHADA Uniform Arbitration Act. The authorities envision complementing the OHADA Treaty by accession to the New York Arbitration Convention of 1958, which will strengthen enforcement provisions and provide greater certainty to investors from non-OHADA signatories.

A second pillar of the legal reform strategy is to adapt national laws to the 2006 constitution and the country's international treaties. This step is important from an institutional development perspective, but it is also crucial for private sector development. Revenue administration and regulation of the legal and financial costs related to challenging decisions by the state are crucial to development of the private sector. The developmental impact of new laws and regulations may benefit from the comments and suggestions offered in public consultations before the laws are published in the official gazette.[9]

Implementation and Enforcement of Commercial Law

Implementation of the law is costly and should be carefully prioritized. The costs associated with legal disputes encourage out-of-court settlement. Such arrangements exist in many forms, including traditional communal arrangements. The extent to which the national authorities may wish to overrule such traditional arrangements is closely related to the peace and security conditions in these areas. In areas where formal procedures are feasible, a ranking of priorities may be warranted.

Arbitration and other alternative methods of resolving disputes are cost-efficient. Although the legislation favors out-of-court settlement and judges and arbitrators may encourage such settlement, no special regulation or practice of professional arbitration, mediation, or conciliation is in place. The reasons for the reluctance to use such mechanisms are not clear, but the cost advantages are well known.[10] A way forward would be to use the opportunity of accession to OHADA as a reason to set up a working group to design a strategy for developing alternative methods of dispute resolution.

The country aims to modernize its formal procedures for settling economic disputes. There are commercial courts in Kinshasa and Lubumbashi, and all 11 commercial capitals are expected to have courts by the end of 2011. Other countries have addressed similar legal issues and found them challenging (see box 5.3). This major institutional development will require substantial financial and human resources. Even under the most favorable circumstances, it will take time to implement the authorities' ambitious plans. Giving priority to a geographic area associated with a

Box 5.3

Judicial Reform

An independent, well-functioning judiciary is vital for combating corruption, enforcing laws, and providing checks and balances on arbitrary power. In many countries, courts are themselves an ineffectual and corrupt arm of the government. Even if judges are above reproach, lawyers, court clerks, and other court officials can add to the web of corruption. The ingredients of reform are many— freedom of information, greater transparency, self-regulation through reform-minded bar associations and law societies, updating of antiquated laws and court procedures, and the independence, competence, and integrity of judicial personnel—but they are complicated to assemble and need time to take root.

Experience suggests that important progress can be made if reforms focus on incentives, institutional relationships, and access to information rather than only on the formal rules, procedures, and expansion of courts. Anticorruption legislation that matches the enforcement capacity of the country, independent supreme audit organizations, and legislative oversight can help.

Source: World Bank 2004.

growth pole may help to establish effective credibility; the effort could then be applied to other growth poles.

The growing engagement of the Democratic Republic of Congo with international legal institutions has been managed with mixed success. The national government and state-owned enterprises have been invited to defend their interests in foreign courts, panels, and institutions, and foreign creditors have tried to assert their rights. These cases are expensive for both contesting parties, and the sums in dispute are typically substantial. Winning a dispute can be financially rewarding and hence may warrant a concentration of resources—financial, institutional, and human—on the Congolese side. Other countries that regularly use international dispute mechanisms, such as Brazil, have established a specialized unit in the Ministry of Justice to defend the national interest in international legal forums.

Technology and Financial Sector Development

The Congolese financial sector is small. Commercial bank assets represent 13 percent of GDP, commercial bank deposits represent 12 percent of GDP, and commercial bank credits represent 7 percent of GDP (as of December 2010). The ratio of commercial bank credit to GDP is one of the lowest in the world despite rapid growth from a small base during 2002–08. Both deposits and loans are largely short term (85 and 88 percent, respectively) and dominated by foreign exchange. The system consists almost completely of commercial banks and microfinance institutions; insurance is a state monopoly. All 20 banks and microfinance institutions are licensed by the central bank (Banque Centrale du Congo).[11]

The absence of a well-developed financial sector has severe economic costs. The 2010 ICA Survey confirmed that private companies consider access to credit as a major constraint to growth. The true economic costs are even higher. Levine (2005, 596) identifies five channels through which financial intermediation contributes to GDP growth: (1) mobilization and pooling of savings, (2) information gathering about possible investments and allocation of capital, (3) monitoring of investments and exertion of corporate governance after finance has been provided, (4) trading, diversification, and management of risk, and (5) ease of exchange of goods and services. GDP growth could benefit from each of these channels, as is recognized by the authorities.

- *Mobilization and pooling of savings.* In the Democratic Republic of Congo only about a tenth of national savings is allocated through the banking system. If the financial sector were more efficient, investment could be allocated to higher-earning projects (Background paper, II.3).
- *Information gathering about possible investments and allocation of capital.* Due to the absence of a competitive banking sector, there is a dearth of information about profitable projects, which limits the flow of domestic and foreign investment.
- *Monitoring of investments and exertion of corporate governance after finance has been provided.* The absence of technical assistance and oversight from financial sector companies has limited the development of a competitive private sector (Background papers, IV.1, IV.2, and IV.3).
- *Trading, diversification, and management of risk.* In the absence of instruments to diversify their risks, some 42 private smelters closed in October 2008 when the price of copper fell below US$4,000 per ton. At the same time, large companies survived, partly because they were more efficient but also because their risks were diversified.

- *Ease of exchange of goods and services.* Transaction costs are elevated in the Democratic Republic of Congo, as illustrated by the cost to transport cash around the country (World Bank 2008).

In border areas, the proximity of banks in neighboring countries reduces these costs. Anecdotal evidence suggests that Congolese companies and individuals (both national and foreign) tend to have foreign bank accounts that allow them to benefit from foreign financial services. In the Great Lakes region, residents maintain such bank accounts in neighboring countries, while in Kinshasa residents rely on accounts in South Africa, East African countries, Belgium, and other developed countries.

The authorities are adopting policies that aim both to address long-term concerns and to provide short-term solutions. Accession to OHADA and tighter banking supervision are expected to address the long-term concerns. The main OHADA provisions that are important for financial sector development are secured transactions, debt recovery and enforcement law, bankruptcy, and accounting standards. Other measures that will have an important long-term impact on financial sector development are the clarification of land rights and the development of a land registry (cadastre), which is envisaged in the government's Doing Business action plan. Tighter enforcement of prudential measures following the bankruptcy of Banque Congolaise in late 2010 may also increase public confidence in the banking system.

The authorities plan to complement these long-term policies with the removal of obstacles to the development of mobile banking by the end of 2011. The technology to use telephones and other telecom equipment for remote payments is internationally available and has contributed to economic growth in other African countries, including Kenya. So far, this technology has not been used in the Democratic Republic of Congo because of legal obstacles. In particular, the law has not been clear about whether these activities should be regulated by the central bank or by the Ministry of Telecommunications and whether a new law is necessary to clarify this. In February 2011 the government announced that these issues had been clarified and could now be addressed by a central bank regulation. The governor of the central bank expects to issue such regulation in 2011. Mobile phone companies may be able to start offering such services starting in 2012.

Mobile banking may spread rapidly, using the widely available mobile phone services network. A total of 17 million mobile phones are being used, substantially higher than the 200,000 bank accounts that are being maintained. Competition among mobile phone companies has reduced costs (Background paper, IV.1), and these companies are expected to compete for the delivery of banking services. However, taxes and other regulatory costs have increased the costs of telecommunications in recent years and may prove to be an important determinant of the penetration of mobile banking.

Mobile banking is expected to provide some of the benefits of financial intermediation, but not all. Mobile banking companies are expected to gather deposits and mobilize savings, payment, and exchange of goods and services as well as allow customers to diversify their economic risks. Mobile banking companies will have less of an advantage in bank lending. Hence the benefits with regard to allocating capital, monitoring investments, and pressuring for better governance may be smaller. Once the legal framework has been clarified, mobile banking services are expected to spread rapidly, providing important economic benefits. However, improving the access of Congolese companies to credit will require effective implementation of the long-term policies listed above.

Employment Growth through Natural Resource Development

The Democratic Republic of Congo's natural resources are projected to make a rapidly increasing contribution to employment growth. Natural resources contribute to employment through three channels: (a) direct employment, (b) backward and forward linkages, and (c) fiscal revenues that may fund employment programs and other public activities. These benefits suggest that it may be in the country's interest to encourage the development of natural resource sectors, not only for their own sake but also for their ability to create employment.

Forestry resources could supply urban centers with competitive, sustainably managed charcoal and wood for construction. But nowadays, due to a weak framework for land use planning, competing interests over land resources, and lack of rational exploitation of natural resources, it is estimated that, by 2030, deforestation could affect more than 12 million to 13 million acres and that forest degradation could affect 21 million to 23 million acres out of an estimated 145 million acres of forests.

Direct and Indirect Employment

The natural resource sectors provide widespread employment to informal "artisanal" miners and loggers and some minimal formal employment in large companies. Artisanal employment generates some 1 million to

2 million jobs, but is vulnerable to price volatility on international markets. In 2008 the authorities requested a program to support former artisanal miners who had lost their livelihood in the wake of the sharp fall in copper and cobalt prices in late 2008 (see box 5.4). Further, artisanal mining offers little opportunity to move up the value chain to more skill-intensive employment.[12] By contrast, sophisticated companies offer opportunities for skilled workers. However, these companies employ modest numbers of workers and are unlikely to be a significant engine of employment growth.

Box 5.4

Experience with Social Programs Implemented in the Context of the 2008–09 Financial Crisis

The Katanga Province, having the country's most important mineral resources, suffered in late 2008 from high unemployment following the collapse of the artisanal mining sector in the wake of the international financial crisis. In 2010 it was estimated that the closing of many artisanal mining operations and the drastic decline in the production of industrial mines had resulted in the loss of about 300,000 jobs. Most of the people affected were young men and women in their 20s and 30s. While Katanga Province has been relatively stable since the 2006 elections, increasing levels of unemployment are putting that stability at risk.

Katanga Labor-Intensive Public Works Project. In 2010 the Labor-Intensive Public Work Project (LIPW) in Katanga became effective. The project was financed by a US$5 million grant from the Peace and Consolidation Fund and later by a US$5 million allocation from the Additional Financing for the Emergency Social Action Project. The project seeks to mitigate the impact of the financial crisis that led to job losses for men and women previously working in the mining sector in Katanga. The project also addresses some infrastructure challenges (by financing subprojects such as road rehabilitation and maintenance, including rehabilitation of the drainage systems of dirt roads, cleaning of canals, unclogging of sewers) in the Katanga Province and promotes the use of labor-intensive methods in public works. The project targets the Kolwezi, Likasi, Lubumbashi, and Sakani corridor where most of the affected people are located.

The project finances both a rehabilitation works component and a training component. The LIPW subprojects are selected on the basis of (a) maximum number of jobs created, (b) percentage of unskilled labor (at least 35 percent of

(continued next page)

Box 5.4 *(continued)*

total costs), (c) simple design to allow quick implementation (maximum project duration of 12 months), (d) total cost of subprojects (not to exceed US$200,000), and (e) percentage of women (minimum 25 percent of unskilled workers). The daily wage for an unskilled worker is US$4, which is the standard rate for unskilled workers in Katanga. The training component finances both (a) training in new skills for artisanal miners and (b) training in LIPW methods for project staff, local executing agencies, and enterprises involved in project execution.

The LIPW project is executed by the Social Fund of the Democratic Republic of Congo (FSRDC), a public agency located under the presidency, which has, since 2004, executed the World Bank–supported Emergency Social Action Project. FSRDC is decentralized and has local offices in all of the country's provincial capitals, including Lubumbashi. The FSRDC selects projects—on a competitive basis—and contracts local executing agencies to act on behalf of the municipal government in the implementation of subprojects. The municipal governments, assisted by the local executing agencies, selects, on a competitive basis, and contracts (a) consulting firms to design the micro projects, prepare the bidding documents with the number of workers and quantity of nonlabor inputs, and supervise implementation and (b) construction firms to implement the subprojects.

Results expected and to date. The US$10 million project is expected to create a minimum of 515,000 person-days of salaried employment through labor-intensive public works, thus improving the living conditions of many female and male artisanal miners and their families in Katanga. Moreover, the 50–60 LIPW subprojects will help to rehabilitate infrastructure in the various mining cities.

By end-February 2011, only a few months after the first group of subprojects had been launched, 12 LIPW subprojects were being implemented and four had been completed. So far, more than 151,500 person-days of salaried employment have been created. Almost 1,800 men and women have been employed for an average period of 85 days. Unskilled labor constitutes, on average, 43 percent of the total cost of a subproject. Women workers represent between 30 and 40 percent of the total number of unskilled workers.

Natural resources may also create employment indirectly through backward and forward linkages Backward linkages consist of demand for goods and services. Forward linkages consist of domestic processing of natural resources. Both artisanal and formal natural resource operations tend to form backward and forward linkages.[13]

Backward linkages are developing rapidly:

- *Transport services*, including trucking and rail services, benefit from the development of mining and forestry activities throughout the country. Nationally transport services grew an estimated 7 percent annually during 2006–10. However, growth was slower in Katanga, as transport companies were unable to meet international standards of mining companies. During the same period, the transport sector in North Kivu expanded 30 percent a year, partly because it was serving artisanal mining and logging with less exacting standards.
- *Construction services* benefited from the natural resource boom during 2001–05. During these years the construction sector expanded much faster than average GDP. Demand for construction services by international companies may provide national contractors with opportunities to acquire new skills and technologies.
- *Security services* remain important. There are no precise data on the value of such services, but professionalization of the sector would allow the enforcement of current standards.

Forward linkages are taking more time to develop. There is no doubt that there are important opportunities in natural resource processing. To benefit, Congolese companies that process these resources need to add value and sell their product at international prices.[14] This typically requires a predictable business environment and reliable infrastructure (power, transport, and telecommunications). Preliminary discussions on this issue are reported in the forthcoming Poverty Reduction Strategy Paper, which suggests creating such conditions in "growth poles," which are confined to specific geographic areas or sectors in the vicinity of rapidly growing mining areas.

How to Promote Natural Resource Development?

Since natural resource development can make important direct and indirect contributions to employment, we review the prospects for growth of this sector. Mining output is projected to grow rapidly in the decade ahead (see figure 5.2); Tenke Fungurume (owned by Freeport McMoran) and the joint venture Secomines are starting operations. These and other operations are expected to boost copper production in the Democratic Republic of Congo to more than 1 million tons, making it once again one of the top five producers in the world. Further, a ban on mining activities in the two Kivu provinces and Maniema was lifted in March 2011.

Figure 5.2   Copper Exports, 2002–18

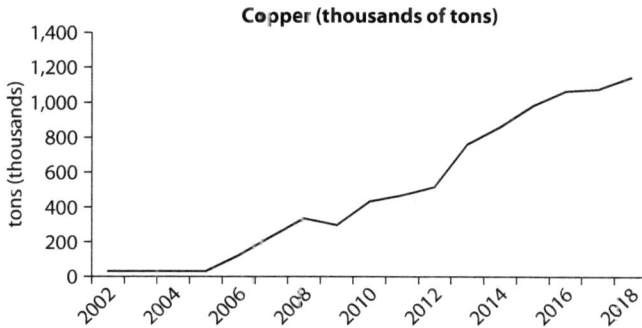

Sources: Congolese authorities and World Bank staff estimates.

The projected expansion in production is impressive but may still fall short of mobilizing the country's full potential. Identified mining resources are modest compared to (a) the country's population and (b) its reputation as a potentially important producer. Since 2002, some new resources have been identified, allowing the Democratic Republic of Congo to enter the league of countries with recently identified resources. The following considerations need to be taken into account:

- *Additional resources are identified in the course of exploitation.* Exploitation is projected to triple during the decade ahead, and it is probable that additional resources will be identified.

- *Identifying additional resources requires public information,* notably a detailed geological survey. Providing such information is costly, but tends to be repaid through the generation of additional tax revenues. Australia estimated the rate of return to be in the range of up to US$5–US$15 for every US$1 invested in public information (Australia House of Representatives 2003).

- *Most of the exploration and exploitation licenses have been allocated—in many cases to state-owned enterprises—but not used.* All exploration licenses for Katanga have been allocated, while some for Kivu and Province Orientale are still in the public domain. Licenses that are allocated but unused are held for speculative purposes; if new resources are discovered, their value increases. In cases where the licensing fees are not being paid, this has a direct fiscal cost over and above discouraging commercial exploration by competing companies.

The Democratic Republic of Congo has taken a strong leadership role in promoting the exploitation of alternative natural resources in the Central Africa region. Climate change has become a strong focus of the government, and a national process for preparing the country to participate in an international mechanism—Reducing Emissions from Deforestation and Forest Degradation (REDD+)—was launched in 2009. This mechanism aims to provide tropical countries with incentives to reduce emissions of greenhouse gases related to deforestation and forest degradation, while providing other benefits, such as poverty reduction and biodiversity conservation. The Democratic Republic of Congo will have to strengthen its technical and institutional capacities in various domains to be able to access the mechanism. Along with other partners, the World Bank is currently providing support to the REDD+ Readiness process in the country—that is, development of required capacities for REDD+, including setting up a legal and institutional framework (land use planning, funds management and benefit sharing, framework to attract private sector investment) and developing a multisectoral strategy. Assuming that the country can successfully develop its readiness program, REDD+ is expected to provide a meaningful flow of revenues to compensate it for revenues forgone as a result of not converting forests to other land uses.

For the immediate future, the main contribution of natural resources to employment will remain indirect, through fiscal revenues. Natural resource sectors tend to be capital intensive and to have minimal direct effects on employment, with the exception of artisanal mining, which is mostly informal and low-skilled employment.[15] The sectors are gradually developing backward linkages, notably in services such as transport. Forward linkages remain a more distant prospect.

Prioritizing the Next Steps by Defining Growth Poles

The Congolese economy is growing rapidly, but employment generation in the formal sector is modest at best. Employment growth will require the development of medium- and small-scale companies. These companies can form linkages with both the large companies that create lots of value added but little employment and the informal and subsistence sector that generates employment but little value added. Development of a vibrant small and medium-size sector requires improved governance, which requires intensive institutional capacity and political commitment, even if realized through public-private partnerships. Hence there is a need for prioritization. The available capacity and other resources are to be allocated to the most urgent tasks, yielding results in the short and long terms. Analytical work on the allocation of infrastructure has demonstrated the benefits of bundling activities; by simultaneously delivering transport, power, and telecom services, the combined effect is larger than the sum of the impact of individual interventions (Foster and Briceño-Garmendia 2010). There are indications that bundling infrastructure services with an improved business environment in growth poles could yield larger benefits than individual interventions. Growth poles may be defined as either sectors or regions.

Such an approach may help to clarify public and private interests. In the Democratic Republic of Congo, public and private interests are closely intertwined, since the scarce human capacity is simultaneously engaged in public and private activities. Combining private and public skills is to be expected, but will be gradually reduced as the country develops; clear separation of public and private activities is one of the hallmarks of economic growth. In the Democratic Republic of Congo, there are many close relations between public and private companies, as, for example, noted in the analysis of the construction sector (Background paper, III.4) or the delivery of trade facilitation activities (Background paper, V.1). Untangling these links will require transparency, monitoring of economic activities, and evaluation of the impact of policy initiatives. Such policies are expected to yield both public and private benefits to all concerned. This requires a careful assessment of the feasibility of promising regions and industries and consequently concentrating institutional and financial resources.

The authorities are committed to providing a level playing field for all firms, but the new Poverty Reduction Strategy Paper also provides support for the growth pole approach, which would be a natural continuation of the authorities' policies and practices. The authorities have placed a high priority on addressing governance issues in the natural resources sector. Similarly, the presidential compound at N'Sele has been designated a special economic zone that can be administered by a private operator. Clarification of land rights through the establishment of a land register has prioritized Kinshasa as well as the cities of Butembo and Beni. A private operator has already managed the generation and distribution of electricity in the city of Tshikapa. Such variable speed in policy formulation and implementation is to be expected in a large country in which the constitution provides provincial and local authorities with significant responsibilities. The analytical work supporting a possible growth pole approach suggests that the benefits of these initiatives could be boosted by concentrating them in a single sector or geographic region.

Notes

1. Executed by agencies reporting to the Ministry of Planning.

2. The importance of the agriculture sector for employment generation and poverty reduction cannot be underestimated. The agriculture sector dominates the Congolese economy in terms of employment. Informal agricultural enterprises employ more than 70 percent of the working population, and agriculture, forestry, and fishing make up more than 40 percent of GDP. Further, the population reliant on agriculture tends to be the most impoverished of the Congolese population, living far below the poverty line. Nevertheless, private actors in the sector appear to be cautiously optimistic about the potential for expansion, while admitting that considerable constraints exist. About 77 percent of firms polled in a survey by the Federation of Congolese Enterprises believe in the potential of the sector to produce growth. At the same time, 11 percent of firms believe that the sector is in a period of contraction, and 14 percent consider it likely that new firms will enter the sector in the short term.

3. See "Buried Treasure," *Professional Engineer*, April 2008. http://www.profeng .com/archive/2008/2107/21070054.htm.

4. The actual number of companies does not give meaningful information because few companies are formally liquidated after they are no longer viable.

5. For example, in both Kinshasa and Bukavu there are competing airports at each side of the border, while in other countries, such as France and Switzerland, the Geneva airport straddles the border and serves both countries.

6. In a rapidly growing economy, such as East Asia, this is less of a problem because debtors are unlikely to default since this would bar them from accessing bank loans. The cost of being excluded from new loans is frequently higher than the cost of default. Creditor rights are enforceable in such circumstances. They are not enforceable in the Democratic Republic of Congo at this time.

7. The Democratic Republic of Congo is an active participant in meetings of the Southern Africa Development Community and the Common Market for East and Southern Africa and may over time decide to join some of the activities of these East African Community members. It benefits from regional assistance from these bodies.

8. Signatories of the OHADA Treaty are Benin, Burkina Faso, Cameroon, the Central African Republic, Chad, Comoros, Republic of Congo, Côte d'Ivoire, Equatorial Guinea, Gabon, Guinea, Guinea-Bissau, Mali, Niger, Senegal, and Togo. In addition to the Legislative Council and the Common Court, the

treaty established a permanent secretariat and a regional training school. See http://www.ohada.com.

9. The legal offices of the Prime Minister's Office and the Presidency review draft laws and regulations for compliance with the constitution and other laws. However, the Parliament and Senate are also involved, sometimes in competition with the government, in drafting "law proposals" that may be opposed to "draft laws," which emanate from the government.

10. International companies regularly use such mechanisms in all countries; in the Democratic Republic of Congo they have used them to settle contract disputes.

11. Another three banks have applied for a banking license, which is pending. In 2010 the central bank increased the minimum capital requirement for new banks from US$5 million, to increase the shock-absorbing capacity of banks, although 13 banks were grandfathered in under the previous legislation and many remain undercapitalized. All banks are required to have a strategic banking partner, which is gradually enforced. In late 2010 the largest commercial bank, Banque Congolaise, was closed by the regulator and is being liquidated, a process that is expected to take up to two years.

12. Following the financial crisis of 2008–09 the Congolese government created work programs for former artisanal miners who had lost their income-generating opportunities as mining prices fell. When mining prices and opportunities recovered, none of the people who had acquired new skills returned to their previous engagement.

13. Katanga has also used trade policies to encourage mining companies to engage in activities that are not related to their expertise. Mining companies were encouraged to develop agricultural activities. These policies may have had some specific benefits given the shortage of managerial and entrepreneurial talent. Thanks to these policies, international agricultural prices did not spike as much in Lubumbashi as in Kinshasa. However, such direct interventions also have costs, as firms were not able to focus on the sector of choice, diverting attention to other activities. An assessment of these policies goes beyond the scope of this report.

14. Production that is established to take advantage of natural resources that are provided below international prices may not benefit the Democratic Republic of Congo; such production tends to disappear as soon as the implicit subsidies of below-cost access to natural resources are withdrawn.

15. There are other exceptions as well. Reforestation, for instance, can be labor intensive and an important source of employment.

CHAPTER 6

How to Sequence Policy Interventions?

The Democratic Republic of Congo has immense development potential and several avenues for policy reform and implementation. Its development potential is evidenced by its endowment of natural and human resources, its geographic size and location, and its sector- and region-specific successes. The main obstacle to realizing this potential is the absence of a broad social governance framework, which has a negative impact on state effectiveness, infrastructure expansion, and private sector development. The Democratic Republic of Congo appears to have begun emerging from two difficult generations of economic stagnation and conflict. The country's leaders, citizens, neighbors, and international development partners are now looking to the future with hope but also realism. In this context, moving forward will mean prioritizing measures that promise to build paths to prosperity and averting the risk of having poor governance derail the possible drivers of sustained and shared growth.

The country's history of governance has roots in its political economy. The elites who are influencing and exercising power are fragmented and narrowly focused. Their lack of trust in the governance system, irrespective of whether that "system" is a political party or the state budget, goes beyond "clientelism." The depth of this mistrust is more extreme and the circle of trusted people is much narrower than in neighboring countries. The lack of a well-respected and functioning state apparatus makes it easier to renege on official agreements, and the risk that powerful groups will resort to violence is significant. The risk that agreements will not be enforced is not limited to particular regions or segments of the country; it is widespread and requires paying attention to political economy issues. These issues evolve over time, as discussed in this chapter.

Progress and Direction

Recent developments offer opportunities for economic reform. The Global and All-Inclusive Peace Agreement of 2002 triggered a gradual restoration of peace in the country. A new constitution was adopted in 2006, with the support of all political parties and stakeholders. The first democratic elections in 40 years were held in 2006, and the second presidential elections are scheduled for November 2011. A large public investment program is being implemented. All legal requirements to implement the framework of the Organization for the Harmonization of Business Law in Africa Treaty have been adopted. Debt relief in 2010 liberated resources for high-priority development activities. The international community continues its deep engagement in the Democratic Republic of Congo, maintaining the largest peacekeeping mission in the world. These developments offer an opportunity to strengthen state effectiveness, deliver infrastructure, and improve the business environment to boost economic growth and employment.

State-owned enterprise reform and a public investment program offer opportunities for growth. State-owned enterprises have traditionally owned and managed the main infrastructure facilities, in many cases supported by legal provisions that stifle competition for the services provided. Results have been limited. A new era is starting, with sector-specific legal reforms, such as the new telecom law, which is encouraging competition by private service providers. Management contracts, public-private partnerships, and full privatization are some of the many arrangements currently under discussion with regard to large infrastructure projects. It is envisaged that these new institutional arrangements will attract private investors and improve maintenance, boosting service delivery. These new business models and the careful selection of investment projects based on transparent criteria are expected to remove important infrastructure obstacles to economic growth.

Challenges

Developing effective state institutions is difficult in a postconflict environment. Institutions establish their credibility gradually over time. But in a postconflict environment, rapid results are needed, and these often require bypassing certain natural steps. For example, the Democratic Republic of Congo established temporary project implementation units in an effort to side-step limited capacity in national institutions. To stabilize, the country must shift from these immediate, short-term arrangements to ones that support the nation's institutional capacity to deliver results. For such a shift to be sustainable, it needs to be grounded in the political economy.

Evolving from a postconflict context to sustainable development is crucial for an economy to thrive. During the immediate postwar period, those influencing and exercising power had little trust in the institutional reforms necessary to achieve growth. Such reforms included establishing a robust and disciplined security service, a meritocratic civil service to which significant decision making could be delegated, and an independent legal and administrative office authorized to sanction predatory behavior by state officials. This climate of mistrust is slowly receding. Those exercising and influencing power feel increasingly comfortable with the national institutions, in part because these institutions are under their control. In sum, institutions are crystallizing as instruments of those exercising and influencing power.

The greater confidence in institutions is conducive to economic growth. State authority and capacity must be reestablished if the economy is to grow. But there is no guarantee that the country's rekindled economic growth will benefit the general population. The good macroeconomic performance during 2010 was based on growth in large-scale mining activities, which contributed only modestly to employment and fiscal revenues. While there are indications of rapid growth in agriculture and in informal sector activities for local markets, there is still no employment growth for skilled youths.

The private sector needs to be freed from pervasive state interference. There is only very modest employment growth in small- and medium-size companies. The analysis suggests that this is the result of excessive interference by state agencies. Public agencies and officials reportedly levy excessive taxes, both formal and informal, on companies, and the smaller companies do not have the political clout or the means to comply and thus fail to thrive. Poor governance in state-sponsored revenue agencies, "trade facilitation" companies, and other organizations that solicit informal payments from small and medium-size companies are the main obstacles to growth in this sector.[1]

Identifying Instruments and Sequencing Their Application

This report identifies four instruments that in some cases have been able to overcome the political economy fragmentation and contribute significantly to growth and employment. These instruments are (1) policy coordination among Congolese interest groups, (2) access to technology, (3) external anchors, and (4) social accountability networks. Matrix 6.1 summarizes the successes and failures that are discussed below.

Policy coordination among Congolese elites is the most effective instrument but also the most challenging. This report and background studies identify cases in which elites have jointly agreed on policies and implemented them effectively. For example, the adoption of the 2006 constitution, the opening of major transport arteries such as the RN4, which connects Kisangani to Uganda, and acceptance of the 2002 decree that allows only four agencies to be present at the border. Each of these three examples has its downside: the 2006 constitution provides legitimacy but not state effectiveness; the transport arteries levy "road maintenance fees" that are not used for this purpose; and the Diagnostic Trade Integration Study published by the government documents the presence of a multitude of agencies at the border. Agreements that build trust by delivering consistent, reliable public services are still not implemented consistently in the Democratic Republic of Congo.

Technologies and external anchors are both effective when fully operational but require national support to get started. We consider three examples in which modern technology has been used to deliver services successfully: (1) employment of a biometric survey of the security forces, (2) the gradual expansion of ATMs to smaller provincial cities, and (3) mobile telephones. Each of these cases began at a time when the country or sector was in disarray. Reforms proceeded largely in the absence of a national partner in the case of telecommunications and with strong assistance from external partners in the cases of the security sector and airport management. Each of these reforms could be applied to similar cases, but heretofore either have not been implemented or have been implemented with long delays. No progress has been made to date on a biometric census in the education sector, reform in the electricity sector is slow at best, and mobile banking services are unlikely to be delivered

Matrix 6.1   Policy Areas and Instruments: Examples of Successes and Failures

Area	Instrument			
	Policy coordination	Technology	External anchor	Social accountability
State building				
Successes	Adoption of OHADA authorizing legislation following sustained support from leading politicians	Biometric census in the security forces	Participation in the United Nations, Bretton Woods, and regional organizations	Free and fair elections in 2006
Unresolved reforms	Murky relations between the national and provincial governments	Biometric census in the education sector	Failure to honor requests for arrests by the International War Crimes Tribunal	Little contact between elected officials and their constituents
Infrastructure				
Successes	Opening up of major roads, such as the RN4 connecting Kisangani to Uganda and the Matadi-Kinshasa road	Automatic teller machines are available in provincial cities	Construction of new infrastructure under a framework agreement with Chinese companies that ensures payment from mining revenues	Collective maintenance of some rural roads by farmers who use these roads to move their products
Unresolved reforms	Poor maintenance of newly opened roads, as road maintenance funds are used for other purposes	Inability to reform the electricity sector, as new technology is not widely used to measure electricity consumption by the public sector	Limited interest of foreign investors in the management contract of Regideso, despite World Bank risk guarantees	Poor maintenance of urban infrastructure, even though maintenance would offset the damage to cars using these roads
Private sector development				
Successes	Decree limiting the number of agencies present at the border	Rapid development of the telecom sector during the postwar period	Absence of exchange control and free use of U.S. dollars	Benefits to agriculture in the vicinity of Kinshasa from cooperation among farmers
Unresolved reforms	Enforcement of the border agency decree	Mobile banking not yet in place because of internal legal obstacles	Enforcement of external dispute settlement mechanism	An absence of cooperatives that could borrow collectively, enforcing creditor rights

Source: Authors.

by end-2011 (although the governor of the central bank and the minister of telecommunications have agreed on regulatory issues). It appears that technology can play an important role in promoting broad-based development, but only if it is actively supported, at least initially, by domestic partners—that is, by strong collective agreements at the political economy level.

The role of domestic partners is even more important for external legal and institutional anchors. We look at three inspiring successes: (1) participation of the Democratic Republic of Congo in the United Nations and the Bretton Woods institutions, (2) the China framework agreement for infrastructure development, and (3) the absence of exchange controls that allow widespread use of the U.S. dollar. The first two are based on the initiative of the Congolese authorities. The third does not require support from the authorities for cash transactions, but the national government has accepted dollar-denominated bank accounts, loans, and other financial contracts as a means of assuring financial stability. The importance of national support is also evidenced by the important cases that remain unresolved, such as (a) the enforcement of arrest warrants by international courts, (b) the need to attract a foreign partner to manage the water utility Regideso, and (c) the enforcement of external dispute settlement panels. These cases remain unresolved either because the authorities have not implemented agreements that parties agreed to voluntarily or because foreign investors fear that the authorities will fail to implement agreements in the future.

In principle, social networks are the most efficient and effective means of assuring government accountability. Social networks empower users to hold service providers accountable. Historically, this stakeholder concept has remained undeveloped in the Democratic Republic of Congo, and even today the examples that we have identified are more conjectural than they are detailed case studies. The 2006 elections were free and fair, but reports indicate that, since then, elected politicians have had only limited contact with their constituents. Farmers and rural communities depend on rural roads, which continue to function, thanks to social networks of users who monitor maintenance. By contrast, urban roads barely function despite the fact that maintenance would more than compensate for the cost of damage to cars.

Social accountability appears to be developing at the local level, while remaining well below par at the national level. The impact of local success stories is illustrated most vividly by the impact of peace and stability on agricultural development. As recently as 2008, agriculture had declined in conflict-affected provinces such as North and South Kivu; in a conflict-affected environment the time horizon is too short for investment in agriculture. However, improvements in security have allowed renewed private investment. The exact terms for such improvements are beyond the scope of this report, but arrangements that are rooted in local conditions seem to have a better chance of success than arrangements that are externally imposed. Such bottom-up growth is important and explains the poverty alleviation gains made during recent years. In addition to bottom-up reforms to boost agriculture, the authorities have used several innovative policy instruments in certain sectors. In some schools, score cards advise parents on the performance of teachers and school administrators, and farmers collectively maintain the rural roads they use (matrix 6.1).

This report illustrates that coalitions have led to some of the most successful reforms. In all cases, coalitions among those exercising or influencing power have played a crucial role in initiating or unleashing key reforms. However, some of these reforms floundered because it is difficult to maintain such coalitions over time. In practice, technology, external anchors, and social accountability have been effective in sustaining the reforms initiated by the Congolese authorities.

This report finds interdependency in reforms that improve state effectiveness, expand infrastructure, and support private sector development. This interdependency goes beyond a virtuous circle in which better infrastructure contributes to private sector development and a stronger state that could make more resources available for infrastructure construction. Matrix 6.2 illustrates that additional infrastructure does not necessarily strengthen private sector development or state authority. For example, the cement sector is dominated by a single producer that influences state policy, illustrating that some firms are too large to be controlled by public policy. Policy makers may want to use an economic cost-benefit analysis to evaluate the impact of alternative policies and investments.

Opportunities to Experiment in a Large, Diverse Country

The size and diversity of the Democratic Republic of Congo offer both challenges and opportunities.[2] Given its provincial structure and the way its constitution was written, the country is able to experiment with different policies in different provinces. This experimentation provides valuable opportunities to share experiences and data. The 2006 constitution

Matrix 6.2 Examples of Interdependencies among Policy Interventions

Interdependency	State capacity	Infrastructure	Private sector development
State capacity			
Reinforcing		An effective state is able to pay its utility bills; in the absence of such payments, reforms of the state, electricity, or water companies are failing.	An effective state is able to provide a predictable regulatory environment conducive to private sector development.
Undermining		Selected state-supported transport companies do not respect weight limits on bridges.	A strong state is able to renege on its private sector contracts with impunity.
Infrastructure			
Reinforcing	Development of the Inga-Katanga power line increases electricity exports, reducing pressures on the balance of payments.		Effective infrastructure boosts private sector development.
Undermining	Construction of bridges and roads connecting to neighboring countries needs to be balanced by institutional arrangements to manage the risks.		Effective infrastructure may lead to deforestation and long-term damage to private sector development.
Private sector development			
Reinforcing	A well-developed private sector contributes to tax revenues and state capacity.	A well-developed private sector could contribute to the construction and management of infrastructure through public-private partnerships.	
Undermining	Collusion among private producers, as is the case in the cement sector, may undermine public policy and economic growth.	An uncontrolled private sector does not observe weight restrictions in planes, leading to crashes.	

Source: Authors.

has placed the delivery of education, health, and agricultural services directly under the purview of the provinces. The decentralized authority for these services does not threaten national unity; rather, the provinces are eager to learn from the experience of their peers.

Experimentation with pilot projects in select provinces may also support the formulation of policy in other provinces. Katanga is experimenting with a public-private partnership for road management. Local taxes are levied effectively in Butembo City (North Kivu), and public services are delivered, offering a possible model for other municipalities. Development partners may have a role to play in bringing officials from the provinces together so that they can learn from each others' experience (see box 6.1).

The national authorities are also using targeted pilot cases to test policy reforms in collaboration with select provinces. Trade facilitation procedures are dominated by national agencies because border control is a national prerogative. All agencies involved in trade facilitation currently support the development of two to three pilot programs. The selected sites include the Kinshasa-Brazzaville border crossing as well as border posts in North and South Kivu. These posts were selected because economic analysis suggests significant prospects for regional integration under the right trade facilitation conditions. Provided that recently started reforms are successful over a one- to two-year period, as measured by increased trade and fiscal revenues, the authorities may decide to implement the same approach at other border posts. Such pilot programs could also be a starting point for a growth pole project (see box 6.2).

Box 6.1

Provincial Budget Management Peer Learning Event

With financial support from the Belgium Poverty Reduction Partnership, since 2009 the World Bank has been supporting the Congolese provincial authorities in their effort to improve budget management practices. In 2011, with financial support from the U.S. Agency for International Development, officials from all provinces were invited to a workshop in Kinshasa, where they discussed and compared the provinces' budget preparation practices. While the presentations and speakers were useful, the informal contacts made between policy makers doing the same task in different provinces will undoubtedly prove to be just as valuable.

Box 6.2

A Growth Pole Pilot Program?

A growth pole pilot program could be used to determine whether coordinated interventions in select areas would have the expected impact. This approach could be used to address the coordination failures that have prevented the application of desirable economic policies. A growth pole region could be small enough to deal with coordination failures. Resource corridors, which better leverage infrastructure as well as provide upstream and downstream linkages around extractive industries, are a natural way to promote growth poles. Over time, the growth pole region would become self-sustainable because all participants would have an interest in the success of the growth pole and would collectively address obstacles to its success. Reaching this self-sustainable phase may be a challenge, however.

It is desirable to anchor the institutional arrangements for growth poles regionally during their start-up phase—say, the first five to seven years. In practice, this could be done through cross-border regional arrangements that involve the East African Community in the Great Lakes region or a similar arrangement in the west or south. Such cross-border arrangements would allow oversight, which would help to create a competitive environment in which small- and medium-size companies could flourish. As these companies develop, they will increasingly foster outward linkages, spreading the benefits geographically.

Even if regionally anchored, growth poles remain a high-risk venture, but the opportunity to create employment for educated youths warrants the risks. Growth poles have existed in Kisangani and other cities, but they collapsed during the 1980s and 1990s. The state was not strong enough to protect its governance from predation. Hence a growth pole approach to economic development will require close supervision and continuous support from senior officials. Such involvement is costly but offers the possibility of gainful employment to millions of young educated Congolese citizens.

Pilot programs require a well-designed monitoring and evaluation program. They are typically developed to test policies and draw lessons that can be applied elsewhere. Lessons can only be drawn if the pilot programs include a monitoring and evaluation component that measures the efficiency, effectiveness, and impact of the interventions. Well-designed pilot initiatives require a requisite level of accommodation by national and Sub-Saharan authorities. Such conditions are even more important to subsequent scaling-up of well-selected initiatives. Increasingly wider coalitions that protect and nurture tangible successes are crucial to significantly boost growth and development in the Democratic Republic of Congo.

Notes

1. The "Weingast paradox" has come to refer to the challenge of establishing an appropriate balance between the state and the private sector, including checks and balances across levels of government. It highlights the dilemma of a strong state in which the government is strong enough to protect property but also strong enough to take it away. Governments will refrain from predatory behavior only if private citizens pay adequate taxes and refrain from raiding one another. People will refrain from predatory behavior only if the government ensures physical security and does not charge unacceptable taxes (Quian and Weingast 1997).

2. The phrase "Unity in Diversity" has been used to characterize Indonesia's approach to development policy; it provides a useful framework for approaching development challenges in the Democratic Republic of Congo.

References

Australia House of Representatives. 2003. "Pre-Competitive Geo-science Data Acquisition." In *Exploring Australia's Future*, ch. 4. Canberra: Standing Committee on Industry and Resources. www.aph.gov.au/house/.

Commission on Growth and Development. 2008. *Commission Report: Strategies for Sustained Growth and Inclusive Development*. Washington, DC: World Bank.

FAO (Food and Agriculture Organization), UNFPA (United Nations Population Fund), and IIASA (International Institute for Applied Systems Analysis). 1984. "Potential Population-Supporting Capacities of Lands in the Developing World." Project INT/75/813. FAO, Rome.

Foster, Vivien, and Cecilia Briceño-Garmendia. 2010. "Africa's Infrastructure: A Time for Transformation." Background paper prepared for the Emerging Markets Forum meeting in Western Cape, South Africa, September 13–15.

Fritz, Verena, Kai Kaiser, and Brian Levy. 2009. *Good Practice Framework: Problem-Driven Governance and Political Economy Analysis*. Washington, DC: World Bank, Poverty Reduction and Economic Management (PREM) Network.

Global Witness. 2009. "'Faced with a Gun, What Can You Do?' War and the Militarization of Mining in Eastern Congo." Global Witness, London, July.

Government of the Democratic Republic of Congo. 2010a. "Diagnostic Trade Integration Study." Kinshasa: Government of the Democratic Republic of Congo. http://enhancedif.org/documents/DTIS%20english%20documents/english/DRC_DTIS_e_August2010.pdf.

————. 2010b. Stratégie de développement de l'enseignement primaire, secondaire et professionnel (2010–2016), Kinshasa (unpublished).

Human Security Report Project. 2010. *Human Security Report 2009/2010: The Causes of Peace and the Shrinking Costs of War.* Vancouver: Human Security Report Project.

IMF (International Monetary Fund). 2010. "Democratic Republic of the Congo: Second Review under the Three-Year Arrangement Under the Extended Credit Facility and Financing Assurances Review—Staff Report; Staff Supplement; Press Release on the Executive Board Discussion; and Statement by the Executive Director for the Democratic Republic of the Congo." IMF, Washington, DC. http://www.imf.org/external/pubs/ft/scr/2011/cr1154.pdf.

IRC (International Rescue Committee). 2007. *Mortality in the Democratic Republic of Congo: An Ongoing Crisis.* New York: IRC. http://www.theirc.org/resource-file/irc-congo-mortality-survey-2007.

Koyame, Mungbalemwe, and John F. Clark. 2002. "The Economic Impact of the Congo War." In *The African Stakes of the Congo War,* ed. John F. Clark. New York: Macmillan.

Levine, Ross. 2005. "Finance and Growth: Theory and Evidence." In *Handbook of Economic Growth,* ed. Philipe Aghion and Steven N. Durlauf, 865–934. Amsterdam: Elsevier Publishers.

Levy, Brian, and Francis Fukuyama. 2010. "Development Strategies: Integrating Governance and Growth." Policy Research Working Paper 5196, World Bank, Washington, DC.

Meditz, Sandra, and Tim Merril. 1994. *A Country Study: Zaire.* Area Handbook Series. Washington, DC: Library of Congress, Federal Research Division.

Ministry of Education of the Democratic Republic of Congo. 2009. *Annuaire statistique de l'enseignement primaire, secondaire et professionnel (2008–2009).* Kinshasa: Ministry of Education.

Pritchett, Lant. 2008. "Implementing Growth Analytics: Motivation, Background, and Implementation." Paper prepared for the Growth Analytics Training Workshop. Department for International Development, London, September 4–5.

Quian, Yingyi, and Barry Weingast. 1997. "Federalism as a Commitment to Preserving Market Incentives." *Journal of Economic Perspectives* 11 (4): 83–92.

Rodrick, Dani. 2008. "Spence Christens a New Washington Consensus." *Economists' Voice* 5 (3, July): 1–3.

Rondinelli, Dennis A. 2006. "Enhancing the Public Administration Capacity of Fragile States and Postconflict Societies: Parallel and Partnership Approaches." U.S. Agency for International Development, Washington, DC.

Temple, Jonathan. 2001. *Growing into Trouble: Indonesia after 1966*. CEPR Discussion Paper 2932 (August). London: Centre for Economic Policy Research.

United Nations. 2009. *Report of the Panel of Experts on the Illegal Exploitation of Natural Resources and Other Forms of Wealth of the Democratic Republic of the Congo*. New York: United Nations.

Wei, Ge. 1999. "Special Economic Zones and the Opening of the Chinese Economy: Some Lessons for Economic Liberalization." *World Development* 27 (7): 1267–85.

World Bank. 2004. *World Development Report 2004: Making Services Work for Poor People*. Washington, DC: World Bank.

———. 2008. "Democratic Republic of Congo Public Expenditure Review." Report 42167-ZR, World Bank, Washington, DC.

———. 2009. World Development Indicators. Washington, DC.

———. 2010a. "DRC: Growth with Governance in the Mineral Sector; Technical Assistance Project." Washington, DC, World Bank, May.

———. 2010b. World Development Indicators. Washington, DC.

———. 2011. *World Development Report 2011: Conflict, Security, and Development*. Washington, DC: World Bank.

Young, Crawford, and Thomas Turner. 1985. *The Rise and Decline of the Zairian State*. Madison, WI: University of Wisconsin Press.

List of Background Papers and Principal Authors, Including Their Affiliation

Volume II. *Historical and Macroeconomic Context*

II.1. *Institutional Dynamics:* Tony Verheijen (World Bank), Faustin Musa Mundedi (University of Kinshasa), and Jean Marie Mutamba (University of Kinshasa)

II.2. *Macroeconomic Policy Constraints:* Dörte Dömeland (World Bank), François Kabuya Kalala (University of Kinshasa), and Mizuho Kida (World Bank)

II.3. *Growth Diagnostics:* Alfie Ulloa (at the time consultant), Markus Scheuermaier (International Finance Corporation), and Claude Baissac (consultant)

II.4. *Economic Growth as an Instrument for Poverty Alleviation:* Virginie Briand (consultant) and Herman Mboyo (consultant)

Volume III. *Sector Studies*

III.1. *Agriculture:* Jean-Claude Chausse (consultant), Thomas Kembola (Ministry of Agriculture), and Robert Ngonde (Ministry of Agriculture)

III.2. *Natural Resource Management:* Chloe Domergue (consultant) and Augustin Mpoyi Mbunga (consultant)

III.3. *Urban Issues:* Claude Baissac (consultant), Anne Sinet (consultant), Alphonse Soh (consultant), and Florence Verdet (consultant)

III.4. *Construction:* Mario Jametti (University of Lugano), Paul Tshiula Tshimanga (University of Kinshasa), and Salim Maloof (United Nations Operational Services)

Volume IV. *Cross-Cutting Issues*

IV.1. *Infrastructure:* George Wolf (at the time World Bank), Fabrice Lusinde (International Finance Corporation), and Julien Galant (International Finance Corporation)

IV.2. *Human Capital and Labor Markets:* Amadou Bachirou Diallo (World Bank), Janine Mans (at the time, World Bank) and Gomez D. Ntoya (Ministry of Planning)

IV.3. *Private Sector Development: Governance, Growth, and Constraints:* Alice Mufungizi (Catholic University of Bukavu) and Alexa Tieman (University of St. Gallen)

Volume V. *Trade and Regional Integration*

V.1. *National Trade Policy and Trade Facilitation Procedures:* Brendan Horton (consultant), Thomas Cantens (at the time, Agence Française de Développement), Philippe Lambrecht (consultant), and Alexa Tieman (University of St. Gallen)

V.2. *Regional Integration in the Great Lakes Region:* Paul Brenton (World Bank), Shiho Nagaki (World Bank), Jean Baptiste Ntagoma (Catholic University of Bukavu), Celestin Bashige (Catholic University of Bukavu)

V.3. *Regional Integration in the Western Corridor:* Marius Brülhart (University of Laussane) and Mombert Hoppe (World Bank)

ECO-AUDIT
Environmental Benefits Statement

The World Bank is committed to preserving endangered forests and natural resources. The Office of the Publisher has chosen to print *Resilience of an African Giant: Boosting Growth and Development in the Democratic Republic of Congo* on recycled paper with 50 percent post-consumer waste, in accordance with the recommended standards for paper usage set by the Green Press Initiative, a nonprofit program supporting publishers in using fiber that is not sourced from endangered forests. For more information, visit www.greenpressinitiative.org.

Saved:
- 4 trees
- 2 million British thermal units of total energy
- 394 pounds of net greenhouse gases (CO_2 equivalent)
- 1,777 gallons of waste water
- 113 pounds of solid waste

green press
INITIATIVE